THE BOUGAINVILLE PHOTOPLAY PROJECT

PAUL DWYER

CURRENCY PRESS
SYDNEY

belvoir

'yes' OPTUS

CURRENCY PLAYS

First published in 2010
by Currency Press Pty Ltd,
PO Box 2287, Strawberry Hills, NSW, 2012, Australia
enquiries@currency.com.au
www.currency.com.au
in association with
Company B Belvoir, Sydney.

Copyright © Paul Dwyer, 2010.

COPYING FOR EDUCATIONAL PURPOSES

The Australian *Copyright Act 1968* (Act) allows a maximum of one chapter or 10% of this book, whichever is the greater, to be copied by any educational institution for its educational purposes provided that that educational institution (or the body that administers it) has given a remuneration notice to Copyright Agency Limited (CAL) under the Act.

For details of the CAL licence for educational institutions contact CAL, Level 15/233 Castlereagh Street, Sydney, NSW, 2000; tel: within Australia 1800 066 844 toll free; outside Australia 61 2 9394 7600; fax: 61 2 9394 7601; email: info@copyright.com.au

COPYING FOR OTHER PURPOSES

Except as permitted under the Act, for example a fair dealing for the purposes of study, research, criticism or review, no part of this book may be reproduced, stored in a retrieval system, or transmitted in any form or by any means without prior written permission. All enquiries should be made to the publisher at the address above.

Any performance or public reading of *The Bougainville Photoplay Project* is forbidden unless a licence has been received from the author or the author's agent. The purchase of this book in no way gives the purchaser the right to perform the play in public, whether by means of a staged production or a reading. All applications for public performance should be addressed to the author c/- Currency Press.

NATIONAL LIBRARY OF AUSTRALIA CIP DATA

Author: Dwyer, Paul.
Title: The Bougainville photoplay project / Paul Dwyer.
ISBN: 9780868198910 (pbk.)
Subjects: Dwyer, Allan–Drama.
Orthopedists–Australia–Biography–Drama.
Peace-building–Papua New Guinea–Bougainville Province–Drama.
Restorative justice–Papua New Guinea–Bougainville Province–Drama.
Bougainville Province (Papua New Guinea)–History–Drama.
Dewey Number: A822.4

Contents

THE BOUGAINVILLE PHOTOPLAY PROJECT   1

Theatre Program at end of playtext

The book has been printed on paper certified by the Programme for the Endorsement of Forest Certification (PEFC). PEFC is committed to sustainable forest management through third party forest certification of responsibly managed forests.

Typeset by Dean Nottle for Currency Press.
Printed by Ligare Book Printers, Riverwood, NSW.
Cover images by Allan Dwyer.
Cover design by Tim Kliendienst.

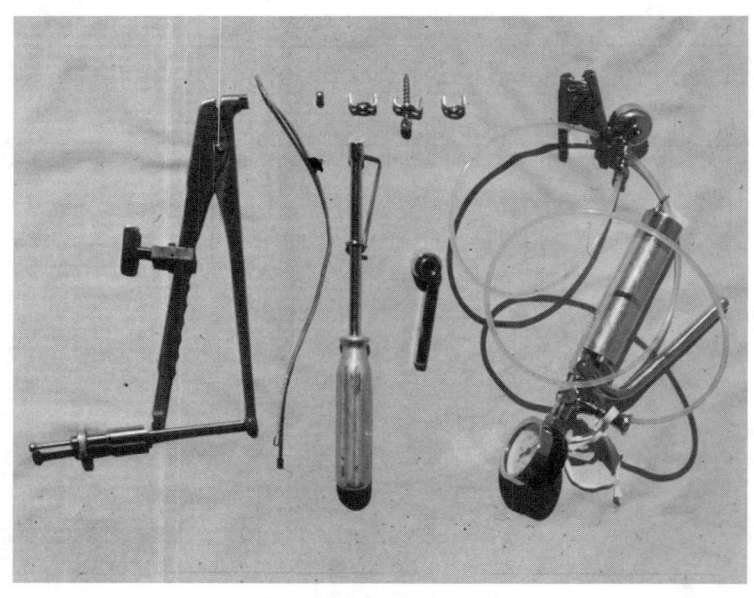

Dr Allan Dwyer's surgical tools.

This published version of *The Bougainville Photoplay Project* was first performed at the National Multicultural Festival Fringe in Canberra in February 2008, with the following participants:

Paul Dwyer	Researcher and Storyteller
David Williams	Director and Stage Manager
Sean Bacon	Video Artist

Subsequent performances have been for the Liveworks Festival at the Performance Space, Sydney (2008); at the Old Fitzroy Theatre, Sydney (2009); and a Mobile States Tour for Performing Lines (2010) which toured to Arts House at North Melbourne Town Hall, Darwin Arts Festival at Browns Mart Theatre, Powerhouse Arts Centre in Brisbane, and Perth Institute of Contemporary Arts.

PLAYWRIGHT'S NOTE

It is worth remembering that this piece has been presented in several different versions, often in venues that lack the facilities of a professionally equipped theatre: a university tutorial room, an art gallery, in the open air underneath a galip nut tree in Bougainville, to name a few. For several years, the 'script' was a few pages of notes, a rough outline for performances that were partly memorised and partly extemporised. Not only the text but also many production elements have been chopped and changed according to the different constraints and potential offered by each performance context and for particular audiences, as well as to take account of new information gleaned along the way. The show's most recent incarnation as an in-theatre performance (from which the following text has been transcribed and to which the staging notes refer) may not be the final form of *The Bougainville Photoplay Project*.

Paul Dwyer

THE PLAYERS

The three members of the theatre company Version 1.0 who play themselves:
  Paul Dwyer, researcher and storyteller
  David Williams, director and stage manager
  Sean Bacon, video artist

PHOTO CREDITS

The images published here are a sample of the photos of Dr Allan Dwyer, or scanned archival documents retrieved from his personal files, which are projected during a performance, together with one photo by the author, Paul Dwyer.

The stage is set as if for a lecture demonstration. Two tables onstage form an L-shape: one holds a selection of books and papers; the other, some tools covered by a drape. There are further research materials and a map of Bougainville displayed on the stage right theatre wall. Above this display are a number of lamps, as if lights for a gallery display.

Upstage, there are two screens upon which a range of materials is projected throughout the performance: excerpts from video documentaries, x-rays and surgical slides, scanned archival documents, family photos, live-feed video focussing on details of the performer's activity, et cetera.

*The performer (*PAUL DWYER*) works mainly around and upon the tables, primarily directly addressing the audience. Two co-performers, the director/stage manager (*DAVID WILLIAMS*) and the video artist (*SEAN BACON*), work from another table, clearly visible on the side of the stage. As the audience enters,* PAUL *is sitting alongside* DAVID *and* SEAN*. The music of a Bougainvillean artist, William Takaku, is playing.*

Music fades as the lights go down. PAUL *makes his entrance 'proper' as the lights come back up. For most of the show, there will also be some low-level light above the audience.*

PREAMBLE: PAUL'S RESEARCH AGENDA

PAUL *enters, carrying a plastic model of a spine and an old globite school case.*

PAUL: Good evening. Welcome. I'm Dr Paul Dwyer from the University of Sydney.

> PAUL *carefully places the spine stage left and the school case stage right.*

A few years ago, I became interested in researching what we might like to think of as the performative aspects of various approaches to reconciliation. Initially, my focus was a process that we have in the New South Wales juvenile justice system called 'youth justice' or 'restorative justice conferencing'.

Basically, one of these conferences is an opportunity for a young offender, say—well, someone like David here—

> PAUL *gestures towards* DAVID *at the tech desk;* DAVID *stands dutifully.*

—to meet face-to-face with the victim of his crime, in the presence of the victim's family and friends, David's family and friends, a police youth liaison officer, perhaps a school teacher, a social worker, that sort of thing. David would give an account of his offending behaviour; he would hear how the victim and other people have been affected by it and then, all of us working together, we would try and find ways in which David could make amends for the harms that he has caused and hopefully be reintegrated into family and community networks. Thanks, David.

> DAVID *sits.*

I really hope it works out for you.

One thing that struck me immediately was the claim made by some restorative justice advocates and certain legal theorists that these newly emerging practices in various Western jurisdictions are, in some sense, a re-discovery or a re-invention of dispute resolution processes that can be found among the New Zealand Maori, among Indigenous Australian peoples, Melanesian peoples and virtually all other 'traditional' cultures and, I do have to say, that's a claim which gets bandied about with scant regard for the relevant anthropological literature.[1]

So you can imagine my excitement when, one evening while I was doing a bit of research (well, actually, just googling away on the internet), I came across the website of a Brother Pat Howley…

> PAUL *moves to the display board stage right, clicks on a lamp and points to the relevant photographs and maps.*

… talking about his work with the NGO Peace Foundation Melanesia, which claimed to be melding Western approaches to restorative justice with the traditional customs of the people here in Bougainville, a region of Papua New Guinea. I thought, 'Bingo! This is it. This is my opportunity to conduct the groundbreaking, cross-cultural, ethnographic research project that the field of restorative justice so desperately needs.' I fired off an email...

THE EMAIL TO BROTHER PAT

PAUL: 'Dear Brother Pat—'

Actually, it can be a little awkward addressing yourself to a Catholic missionary when you yourself are a badly-lapsed Catholic, but anyway...

'Dear Brother Pat,

'I wonder if you could offer some advice about the practicalities of studying restorative justice in action on Bougainville. I'm an academic working in the Department of Performance Studies in the Arts Faculty at Sydney University.

'I'm looking to develop a post-doctoral research project into restorative justice—'

You might notice I put a bit of stress on the word 'post-doctoral'. I didn't want him thinking I'm some neophyte researcher, you know I've got a few runs on the board.

'—ideally by comparing and contrasting the way it works in an urban, Western setting, like the New South Wales juvenile justice system, to the way it looks in a rapidly changing Melanesian society.'

Open parentheses: '(There's a significant sentimental reason for focussing on Bougainville which I'll come back to in a moment.)' Close parentheses.

'I was certainly struck by the dramatic images from the reconciliation ceremony at Hahon in Bougainville which were shown recently in the documentary film *Breaking Bows and Arrows*—'

VIDEO INTERLUDE: BREAKING BOWS AND ARROWS

PAUL: And we might just pause here for a moment to have a look at a brief excerpt from this excellent documentary film, *Breaking Bows and Arrows*, by Liz Thompson.[2] I think it will give us all a shared context for the weave of stories that are to follow.

PAUL *looks towards* SEAN *at the tech desk.*

So, Sean, you have that clip from Liz Thompson's film all ready to go, don't you?

SEAN *mumbles something in the affirmative.*

Wonderful. You see, ladies and gentleman, Sean is not a young offender. Sean is an artist.

The video clip comes up with aerial shots of Bougainville's mountainous landscape and the sound of women singing 'There are people crying; there are people dying. Who is responsible?'

While the video plays, PAUL *is quietly changing into shorts, cheap t-shirt and sandals.*

VIDEO VOICEOVER: On Bougainville Island in Papua New Guinea, people have turned to tradition in search of healing. Unlike South Africa where the Truth and Reconciliation Commission is working to unite a broken community, Bougainvilleans are taking part in their own reconciliation ceremonies after a bitter war divided them. One of the catalysts to the war came in the 1960s when Australia encouraged mining in the colonial territory of Bougainville. Landowners were offered a meagre sum for their land on which Australian company CRA planned to develop one of the largest open-cut copper mines in the world. There was serious opposition to the proposal.

The video cuts to archival black-and-white interview footage.

INTERVIEWEE 1: [*a Bougainvillean man*] Yes, the government will not take our land.

INTERVIEWEE 2: [*another Bougainvillean man*] It's better for us to— Government have to kill us, to take our lands.

REPORTER: The government will have to kill you?

INTERVIEWEE 2: Yeah.

REPORTER: To take your land?

INTERVIEWEE 2: Yes.

BARRY MIDDLEMISS: [*a white man resident in Bougainville*] If the government persists in its arrogant attitude and its demands on the people, there is going to be a guerrilla style of warfare here shortly.

THE BOUGAINVILLE PHOTOPLAY PROJECT

VOICEOVER: The government took little heed of the discontent and Bougainville Copper Mine was established. By the time Papua New Guinea became independent in 1975 the mine was responsible for nearly half the country's export earnings. The landowners' grievances intensified. Many Bougainvilleans hoped to become independent of mainland Papua New Guinea and these aspirations had been ignored. A meagre share of the mine's profits and serious environmental degradation finally led to an uprising in 1989 and the Bougainville Revolutionary Army, the BRA, came into existence. The government's response was to send in the Papua New Guinea Defence Force, the PNGDF, whose violence further aggravated the situation.

MARCELINE TUNIM: [*Bougainvillean peace activist*] When PNG army killed him, when the man who was looking after them all came in, he took the tray over; my mother got my brother's blood and she began to paint it all over her face, her head. She was also drinking from it but then we had to push her away from what she was doing and she, she was nearly crazy and I don't know what this PNG army thought when he saw us because he was very silent then. All of my brother's bones were crushed. We could see that a hammer was used to break the bones. Something very hard was thrown on his teeth; it was the barrel of the gun. He had knife wounds all over his body. All his tendons were cut with a sharp object and a very big hole went right through his heart. Then because my brothers saw the wounds, they must do something and fight against this mighty army. That is why they join the BRA. And they are really hard core because they have seen blood pour out of my brother who is really innocent.

VOICEOVER: The mine was closed and the conflict became a struggle for independence. A decade-long secessionist war began. The war became more complex and insidious when a third element emerged in the form of the Resistance. The Resistance was made up of Bougainvilleans who supported and assisted the Papua New Guinea Defence Force in its efforts to suppress the BRA.

MARCELINE TUNIM: The Resistance were paid big money by PNG government to help them track down BRA because PNG army knew that on their own they would never find BRA. Because this is the land of BRA, the mountains are theirs. And they do not know how to get into the mountains to beat BRA so they use Resistance as the shield, as the human shield.

VOICEOVER: The Papua New Guinea government imposed a blockade in which all food, communications and medical supplies were stopped. An estimated fifteen to twenty thousand people died during the crisis and Bougainville's infrastructure was almost entirely destroyed. In 1998, a ceasefire was finally signed. However clans, communities and families are bitterly divided. There is hope that culturally-based reconciliation ceremonies will bring the healing required as Bougainville builds a new future.

End of video excerpt.

Lights back up on PAUL.

TRAVEL PREPARATIONS

PAUL: The response to my email was a very warm invitation to travel around Bougainville with the local area coordinators of Peace Foundation Melanesia. I made preparations for a brief 'reconnaissance field trip'…

PAUL *points to his new costume.*

… my ethnographic fieldwork outfit. And the Lonely Planet Guidebook:

'North Solomons Province (Bougainville): You should seek the advice of your country's diplomatic representatives in PNG or your department of foreign affairs before making any travel plans. The whole region is besieged by the crisis. It is a messy guerilla war on a large mountainous and thickly jungled island and people are getting killed. Stay off Bougainville unless you're travelling with a local person who knows exactly what they're doing—and, even then, think about it.'[3]

Okay, well that's written in 1998; I'm travelling in 2004. The crisis is over. I should be fine. But I did think it might just help to learn how to communicate a little more effectively with the locals. Time was short; I hit the books as hard as I could.

A LANGUAGE LESSON

The soundtrack of a Tok Pisin language course blares out over the theatre's PA system.

VOICEOVER: A New Course in Tok Pisin, Unit 3.[4] Vocabulary drills, exercise 4: simple substitution. Frame: *Raskol i kam stilim kaset long kar... Kaset...*

> PAUL *repeats each frame sentence before translating for the audience.*

PAUL: *Raskol i kam stilim kaset long kar.* The rascal stole a cassette from the car.

VOICEOVER: *Raskol i kam stilim kaset long kar... Teprikoda...*

PAUL: *Raskol i kam stilim teprikoda long kar.* The rascal stole a tape recorder from the car.

VOICEOVER: *Raskol i kam stilim teprikoda long kar... Vidiorikoda...*

PAUL: *Raskol i kam stilim vidiorikoda long kar.* The rascal stole a video recorder from the car.

VOICEOVER: *Raskol i kam stilim vidiorikoda long kar... Ol samting bilong mi...*

PAUL: *Raskol i kam stilim ol samting bilong mi long kar.* The rascal stole all of my things from the car.

VOICEOVER: *Raskol i kam stilim ol samting bilong mi long kar... Olgeta samting...*

PAUL: *Raskol i kam stilim olgeta samting long kar.* The rascal stole everything from the car.

VOICEOVER: *Raskol i kam stilim olgeta samting long kar...* Sub-section 3.4: evaluation exercise. Listen to the following Tok Pisin sentences and say what they mean in English. Where necessary put each in the past tense. Ready? *Olgeta manmeri i no bihainim olgeta lo.*

PAUL: *Olgeta manmeri i no bihainim olgeta lo...* Not all men and women follow all the laws.

VOICEOVER: No-one followed all the laws... *Ol raskol i bung long Fomil. Bung pinis ol i go long Boroko.*

PAUL: Okay, this is past tense... *Ol raskol i bung long Fomil*... The rascals met at Four Mile... *Bung pinis*... After their meeting... They went to Boroko.

VOICEOVER: The rascals gathered together at Four Mile. After that, they went to Boroko... *Ol rabisman i no laikim ol politisen.*

PAUL: *Ol rabisman i no laikim ol politisen.* This is present tense. Poor people don't like politicians.

VOICEOVER: Poor people don't like politicians... *Olgeta rida i sindaun we?*

PAUL: *Olgeta rida i sindaun we?* Where are all the readers sitting?

VOICEOVER: Where did all the readers sit down?

PAUL: I'm not sure why that's past.

VOICEOVER: *Yupela i gat strongpela drink insait long woksop o...?*

PAUL: *Yupela i gat strongpela drink insait long woksop o...?* Have you people got hard liquor in your workshop or...?

VOICEOVER: Did you (plural) have hard liquor inside your workshop or...?

PAUL: I don't know why he puts that in the past tense there.

VOICEOVER: *Dispela dok i kakai pinis ogleta kakai bilong karakuk ya.*

PAUL: *Dispela dok i kaikai pinis*—so this is definitely past tense—*olgeta kaikai bilong kakaruk ya*... This dog has eaten all of this chicken's food.

VOICEOVER: This dog ate all the food belonging to this chicken.

> PAUL *jumps into storytelling mode; a map of Bougainville is projected on-screen and a slow panning shot traces a journey down the coastline.*

ROADBLOCK STORY

PAUL: So I'm in the back of a ute with people from Peace Foundation Melanesia and about a dozen other people who are just piled in, hitching a ride. We've come to a roadblock at Aropa airstrip, just south of Arawa. The roadblock is manned by members of the

Me'kamui Defence Force. Now, they're very hard core. When the other Bougainville Revolutionary Army people came down out of the mountains and joined the peace process, the Me'kamui boys stayed up there. They held on to their guns. They set up a No Go Zone all around the Panguna mine area which sometimes reaches, as it did here, down to the coast. Now, relations between the Me'kamui boys and the ex-BRA can be pretty dicey. I mean I did learn—though happily this was only with hindsight—that there had been a shootout at this particular roadblock not long before and a couple of people had been killed. Certainly, there had been some discussion amongst our group about how we would go negotiating through this roadblock but then I was told, 'Don't worry, it's alright. Bernard, our driver, is a cousin (or maybe it was a brother-in-law or something) of Captain Amos the Me'kamui Defence Force commander who is running the roadblock, so…' But I'm still thinking this is not a good look. In the front of the truck, you've got a woman called Rhoda. She's from the Port Moresby office of Peace Foundation Melanesia, so she's what the Bougainvilleans might call a '*redskin meri*'. '*Redskin*'—that's a derogatory term which Bougainvilleans sometimes use to describe people from the mainland and then the '*redskins*' sometimes call the Bougainvilleans 'black bastards' so there's possibly a bit of tension there and then you've got this '*waitpela* man' in the back but, you know, it seems to be going okay. Captain Amos is talking to Rhoda, there's a nod of the head and now he's coming around to talk to me but Bernard, our driver, has not told me what my alibi is…

'*Yu pris?* Are you a priest?'
'*Nogat! Mi no pris.* No. I'm not a priest.'
'*Bilong wanim yu kam long Bogenvil?* So what are you doing in Bougainville?'

And that's a really tough question to answer if you're trying to do groundbreaking cross-cultural ethnographic research!

'Ah… *Mi wokabout tasol.* I'm just having a little walk around…'

I've got my happy ethnographer's smile on but it's not really working. People from Peace Foundation Melanesia and the other travellers are all jumping in, trying to help me out…

'*No, em orait. Yu no inap wori. Dispela waitpela man em pikinini bilong dokta husat i bin kam long Bogenvil long taim bipo...*'

They're talking about my father...

'*Bipo long taim bilong crisis. Papa bilong em bin kam bilong wokim sampela operesen long ol haus sik bilong ol katolik mission...*'

He did some operations...

'*Bilong stretim ol bun bilong ol manmeri husat i no inap wokabout gut tumas...*'

He helped people to walk or something...

'*Nau dispela waitpela man, pikinini bilong dispela dokta ya, em laik kam long Bogenvil tu, nau go raun raun long ol ples we papa bilong em bin stap long taim bipo, na bung wantaim ol manmeri husat papa bilong em bin save halivim...*'

And the idea that I might be making some kind of pilgrimage to visit places where my father had been before—well, that seemed to make sense to Captain Amos and he just waved us on...

Open parentheses.

PARIS AND LES SCOLIOSES

PAUL: This part of the story begins fifteen years ago, when I was a student at the University of Paris, boarding with a woman called Brigitte Angays. Brigitte is a translator and interpreter so it wasn't unusual to come home and find a pile of reference books lying on the kitchen table that Brigitte would have borrowed from the library in order to brush up on some area of technical vocabulary. One day I came home and there were some books there about orthopaedic surgery, in particular about the treatment of scoliosis, which is a severe and potentially fatal condition where the spine becomes twisted and curved. And I remembered that this was the area of medicine in which my father, who was an orthopaedic surgeon, had specialised.

Being academically inclined, of course I went straight to the back of the book to check out the bibliography and there is indeed a reference to Dwyer, Newton and Sherwood: 'An anterior approach to scoliosis: a preliminary report'. That's published in *The Journal of Clinical*

Orthopaedics.⁵ There's quite a helpful diagram, some pictures of surgical implements and this brief explanation…

> DAVID *wheels one half of the L-shaped table set-up, on which* PAUL *is sitting, downstage while* PAUL *recites in French.*

'*Les techniques d'arthrodèses antérieures, dans le traitement des scolioses, initiées par Dwyer, sont d'acquisition encore récente et ne sont pas encore de pratique courante sauf dans certains services. Leurs indications sont limitées et encore controversées.*'⁶

They're saying it's quite a controversial, radical approach. As I understand it, up to that point, the main way of operating on scoliosis was to come from the patient's back and to work on the concave side of the spinal curvature, using a fixed metal rod to push apart the ends of the curve. But my father's approach was to get the patient lying on their side…

> PAUL *lies on the table, mimicking the diagram in the French book; live-feed video from overhead is projected on the screen;* DAVID *attends to* PAUL *in the manner of a medical intern.*

… to make an incision, I think about here please, David…

> DAVID *draws a mark along* PAUL*'s rib cage.*

… to remove some ribs, go down through the chest cavity and access the spinal curvature from the convex side. And, using a system of screws and flexible cabling, you can pull together the vertebrae at that point, the result being a quicker and more dramatic straightening of the curve as the patient's spine continues to grow. Of course, it's not the appropriate intervention in all cases and it is, technically, a difficult operation.

ORTHOPAEDIC SURGERY DEMO

DAVID *becomes* PAUL*'s assistant as they move to the remaining half of what had been the L-shaped table, now the 'operating table', upstage left.* DAVID *reveals a number of surgical instruments and a collection of old vertebrae; again, a live-feed video projects close-up details of the following activity onto one of the upstage screens.*

PAUL: If I could just show you this specimen—actually, I found these bones in the wardrobe of my old bedroom at Mum's house; Dad would use them for his lecture-demonstrations…

Having exposed the spine you put a staple around the point at which you want to start correcting the curve and then a screw goes down into the vertebra. (I won't screw this all the way down because these bones are now quite brittle.) Then, we move to the next vertebra… Staple… Screw…

Next we have this titanium cable, designed to pass through holes that are in the heads of the screws but in one direction only. The other end of the cable goes onto this tensioning device. I think you can see these grooves here: each one of these lines corresponds to a certain amount of pounds per square inch of pressure, so you can calibrate quite carefully how much tension you want to put through the cable…

Then, finally, with what my father called his 'swaging' device, you crimp the screw heads so that the cable can't slip back through.

Thank you, David. If you could close for me…

DAVID *tidies up.*

PRE-OP AND POST-OP POWERPOINT DISPLAY

PAUL: As I say, it's technically very difficult surgery. You're going close to major organs—the heart, the lungs, the great vessels, the spinal cord. You would obviously want to be confident of achieving some good outcomes before you ripped open a great gaping wound in a person's chest. We have some of my father's old surgical slides and x-rays that I would like to show but I should warn you the first couple of images are quite graphic. So what I thought we could do is this: I will give a verbal description of what's in the images before I ask Sean, our resident artist, to put them up on the big screen. That way you can decide for yourselves whether tonight is the night for coming to grips with the realities of orthopaedic surgery. Does that sound reasonable? That's my ethical commitment to you, if you like.

Okay, so with those caveats in place, the first image—which is quite red—will show a patient's chest opened up; the spine is exposed and there is a screw going down into one of the vertebrae… Thank you, Sean.

SEAN *puts up surgery image 1.*

For those of you who are looking, you'll see there is a gap on either side of this vertebra. That is because the intervertebral disks have been removed which is what allows the possibility for some play so that you can start to straighten the spine.

The next image will show the tensioning device coming down onto the lead screw head… Thank you, Sean.

Surgery image 2.

You can see how the gap between these two vertebrae has closed up now. The vertebrae will start to fuse together quite quickly which means that, yes, the person will have a somewhat stiff back at this point but they will be able to walk.

Okay, that's it for the technicolour images. Moving now into some black-and-white x-rays, firstly, we'll see a pre-operative slide… Thanks, Sean.

Image.

This is an extreme scoliotic curvature. I was speaking to a Dr John Stephen who worked with my father at the Mater Hospital in Sydney, and he explained that this patient is going to die if not operated on. Eventually the spine will twist so much that it starts to crush the major organs. The patient would die of asphyxiation as much as anything else. So here's the post-op x-ray…

Image.

Still a way to go but obviously a dramatic improvement. John Stephen said this would have been about thirteen hours of surgery. Apparently, sometimes they would have to take a break; they'd go out onto the balcony of the Mater Hospital and have a cup of tea which is, you know, a nice image, but it does freak you out a little when you think about the patient still lying there on the table!

Now we've got some black-and-white photographs which show, firstly, a woman's back before the operation…

Image.

… and the same woman's back immediately after the operation…

Image.

Thank you, Sean.

So that was a part of my father's work.

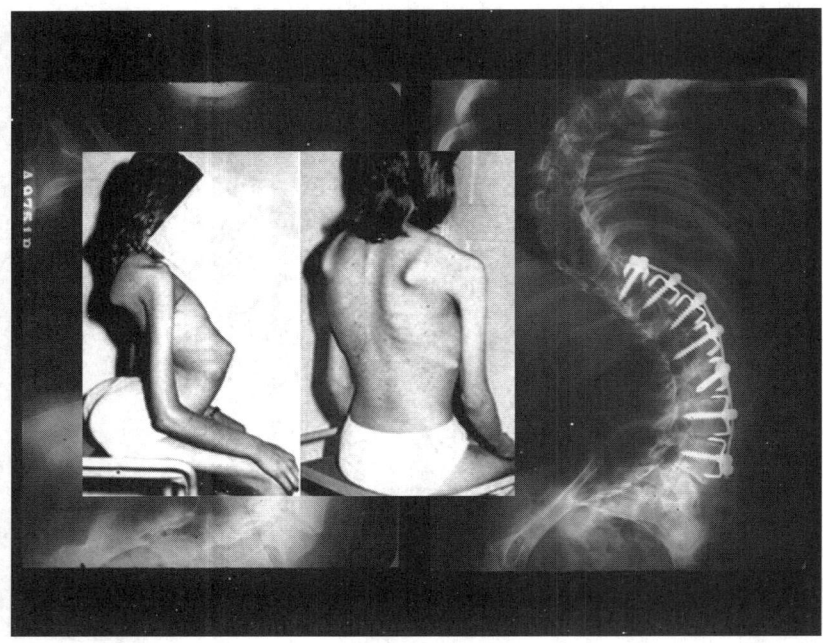

THE 'JOHN BERGER QUESTIONS'

PAUL: While I was studying in Paris, I also started reading a beautiful book by John Berger called *A Fortunate Man: The Story of a Country Doctor*.[7] It's a photo-essay in which Berger and his collaborator, Jean Mohr, a photographer, are trying to understand the significance of a doctor's work in the life of the small, rural community where the doctor has settled into general practice. Towards the end of the book, Berger starts struggling with how to sum up the doctor's record of achievement. How are we meant to do this? Do we try some kind of quantitative measure? Say, Dr X has only treated one hundred patients whereas Dr Y has treated a thousand? But what if Dr Y was occasionally careless? How would you factor that into the equation? Perhaps, Berger suggests, we should use a qualitative measure instead?

'How does the cure of a serious illness compare in value to one of the better poems of a minor poet? How does making a correct but extremely difficult diagnosis compare with painting a great canvas?'

They're impossible questions but this is precisely Berger's point:

'We in our society do not know how to acknowledge, [... or even how] to imaginatively try to take the measure of a man doing no more and no less than easing—and occasionally saving—the lives of a few thousand of our contemporaries. Naturally, we count it, in principle, a good thing. But fully to take the measure of it, we have to come to some conclusion about the value of these lives to us now.'

MUM'S ATTIC

PAUL: After I got back from Paris—so this is in 1996—there was this period where I'd keep going around to Mum's house and, while she'd be making a cup of tea, I'd go sneaking up into the attic because, basically, you can find whatever you need in my mother's attic (and now she loves this show because she can see all the things from her attic are slowly migrating to my attic).

> PAUL *moves to the display board, clicks on another light and indicates the relevant documents; there are also some old notebooks and boxes retrieved from his mother's attic.*

I found all these old journal articles, news clippings and photos about my father's work. You go through this stuff and it becomes very clear that, by the early 1960s, he's at the height of his powers as an orthopaedic surgeon. He's being invited all around the world to conferences and major teaching hospitals to demonstrate his techniques.

But what none of these stories mention—and what, to be honest, I had almost completely forgotten myself until I landed on Br Pat Howley's website—was that during this very same period Dad was making a series of trips to Bougainville to work pro bono in the small Catholic mission hospitals up there.

So just before my brief reconnaissance field trip in 2004, I went foraging again in Mum's attic and I found this box of old Kodachrome slides from my father's trips to Bougainville in 1962, 1966 and 1969…

> PAUL *takes the box of slides to the table and opens it up before moving to the old globite school case which he also opens.*

… and also Dad's old slide projector, still in the same case it was in about forty years ago and still basically in the same condition.

I remember when we were kids, if there was nothing good on television and if Dad was preparing for a lecture or if he was about to go off on one of his trips overseas, we'd be allowed to sit and watch him preparing a slide show pretty much along the lines of what Sean was just showing us a moment ago.

> PAUL *is setting up and preparing to operate his father's old slide projector.*

So I'm there at my mum's house, I'm about to go to Bougainville for the first time, and I've discovered these slides. I made a little selection, got them digitised and printed onto cards and made up a little booklet, just on spec, so that I would be able to show Dad's photos to people I might meet in Bougainville. I would like to show these same slides to you now and share some of the reactions the people in Bougainville had to them when I was there in 2004.

FAMILY SLIDE SHOW

Slide: 'Me and the Boys'.

PAUL: So there's Dad in the middle of a river which runs behind the '*haus sik*', the little hospital, at Tearouki on the north-east coast of the main island of Bougainville. You can see that he has four boys with him—those are my four eldest siblings. The way I understand it is that Dad came home one day in 1962 and said, 'Nano,' (that's my mum's name) 'Nano, there's a great medical need in the missions—I'm going to go to Bougainville for about two months.' At which point Mum gently reminded him that they had eight children and she didn't fancy looking after them all on her own. To which his response was, 'Right, okay, well how about you take four and I take four?'

THE BOUGAINVILLE PHOTOPLAY PROJECT

Slide: 'Catch of the day'.

My brothers still recall the highlights of their trip—that's Damien on the left of screen, Garrett next to him, then Denis and Terry on the right. Dad's caption for this photo is 'Catch of the Day' and in 2004 I was lucky enough to meet the man who cooked that fish—he described my brothers as 'lively'.

Of course when my brothers talk about these trips now they are looking back as adults, whereas I wanted to know what was it like for them at the time. So I was very excited when Damien managed to find, in his attic, this little diary—my mother apparently gave one of these books to each of the boys and said, 'You must record your observations as you travel around'. Terry was the only one who did as he was told and then somehow the diary ended up in Damien's attic, not Terry's, but anyway... Herewith, the thoughts of a thirteen-year-old Australian boy on his way to Bougainville in 1962:

'From Brisbane to Port Moresby seemed very long. While we were approaching Moresby we had our breakfast. Then we ran into some cloud. Moresby appeared dry but it was very humid at the airport. The trip from Moresby to Lae seemed very short and pleasant. On this stretch we all had windows. Lae seemed much more pleasant then Moresby and everywhere there were all sorts of flowers. It was here that Damien discovered the loss of his jacket. I arranged for the TAA people to forward it to Bougainville. Here at Lae we changed planes. We now were in a DC3. All of us had windows. After a while, we were over the Bismarck Sea. For a while I fell asleep. When I woke up I took some pictures and then dozed off. This was an uncomfortable journey towards its end because of the high humidity. My pants were wet with perspiration. At Rabaul, we met Mr Chan and spent the day at the native market, the native hospital, the docks and driving around. From now on I am going to use my shorts. Next we flew to Buka where we met Bishop Lemay. We went to Hahela mission where we met the natives in force. We then crossed Buka Passage and thence to Tsiroge. Under the care of Mr Peter Fenton, we boarded the *St Joseph*. At first the sea was calm, but later we had some good rough stuff and arrived at Tearouki.'

Slide: Arrival at Tearouki.

Arrival at Tearouki, 1962.

And there they are on arrival at Tearouki. The nun on the left of screen is, I believe, Sister Mary Leo—by all accounts an outstanding general surgeon. The other nun is Sister Therese-Anne, an anesthetist. And you can see that Terry, who is standing in front of Dad, has now got his shorts on.

The great thing about Terry's diary is that you realise he is narrating events of which my father was taking photographs. He describes, for instance, a walk up into the hills behind Tearouki, to the village of Pateaveave.

Slide: Fr McConville and Denis at Pateaveave.

My father's caption for this photo…

PAUL *points to the relevant details in the slide.*

… reads: 'Denis and Fr McConville at Pateaveave'. He doesn't mention Damien, who's here, but, to be honest, it was only about the fourth or fifth time I looked at this slide that I noticed what else my father and I were missing: it's the presence of this Bougainvillean man in the corner. His head is turned. He's looking straight back down the lens of the camera that my father must have been holding. I've often wondered what this man saw when he looked at my father, how he would have made sense of my father's presence there. Certainly, from this point on, it became much more obvious that my brothers and the other white people are nearly always occupying the middle of the frame in my father's photographs. Obviously, his focus is to document the boys' holiday experience but this does have the effect, figuratively at least, of pushing Bougainvillean people to the margins.

Slide: The assembled villagers of Pateaveave.

The only time I could find photographs with Bougainvillean people in the centre of the frame, it was always a group shot like this. Here are the villagers of Pateaveave gathered en masse, presumably so that the visiting dignitary, my father, could take a photograph.

Terry's diary again: 'When it rains here, it really rains. One gets used to the fauna and flora quickly and thinks he is in Australia. However, the main contrasts are provided by the natives and malaria.'

And this bit I love: 'Nurse Roddy has got her choir singing "Dixie" and it is sung very well, though it seems strangely out of place.'

Denis and Fr McConville at Pateaveave, 1962.

Slide: The Girls Choir at Tarlena.

In 1966, my father made his second trip to Bougainville and I have been told that this is the Tarlena Girls High School Choir of that year, most probably rehearsing for the Hanahan Choral Festival. When I showed this photograph to people in Bougainville in 2004, they would always laugh and go, 'Oh right, yeah, colonial style', I guess in reference to the girls' hairstyles and resplendent uniforms. But, going back through Dad's photographs, I discovered he had taken a reverse angle photograph of this same event…

Slide: Reverse angle shot of the white folk watching the choir.

… and I think 'colonial style' is also this kind of relationship, isn't it? That's the white missionaries on the verandah of the priest's house, watching the girls while they rehearse out in the hot sun.

For his 1966 trip—I guess because things had gone so swimmingly well with the four boys and Mum was keen to continue the precedent that had been set—my father decided to take with him my siblings Number Five and Number Six, my sister Mary and my brother Patrick. There's one photograph of Mary from this trip…

Slide: Mary with the nuns at Chabai, 1966.

… which is very special, not just because of Mary's gorgeous pink blouse and floral skirt but because this is near a convent at a place called Chabai, on the north-west coast of Bougainville's main island. I also visited Chabai in 2004; the convent is still there. I also met a group of nuns and I also took a photograph. Without realising it, I was standing in almost exactly the same spot as my father must have been standing when he took his photograph.

> *On the screen,* PAUL's *photo of the nuns at Chabai in 2004 fades in slowly over the top of the slide of Mary and the nuns in 1966.* PAUL *turns off his dad's slide projector.*

CONVERSATIONS AT CHABAI AND THE 'JIM HARDING CORRESPONDENCE'

PAUL: The nuns in my photo are all Melanesian women of course: this is Sister Lorraine Garasu (a Bougainvillean living national treasure,

Tarlena Girls High School Choir (above) and colonial spectators (below), 1966.

Above: Mary and the nuns at Chabai, 1966.
Below: Nuns at Chabai, 2004

a very important person in the peace process), Sister Margaret, Sister Elizabeth, and here, on the right, is Sister Catherine Mona, the head of the congregation. I spent a fantastic evening with these women, swapping stories, looking at photographs. They helped me identify some of the girls from the Tarlena High School Choir of 1966.

The projection of an annotated photocopy of the Tarlena Choir photo comes up on screen.

So this is Teresa Peritonoel—I'm told that she's now a teacher at Tinputz. This woman is Hortense Tanei—she worked for a long time as a secretary in Moresby and now she's back in the village of Siara, looking after her grandchildren. On the right hand side, that's Anna Wara who's now a nurse at Torokina. Next to her, we think that's Veronica Kili. And then there was this great moment where the younger nuns started giggling and they pushed the book of photos across to Sister Catherine Mona, the head of their congregation, and she goes, 'Oh yeah… um… that's… me!' You can see her there in the third row.

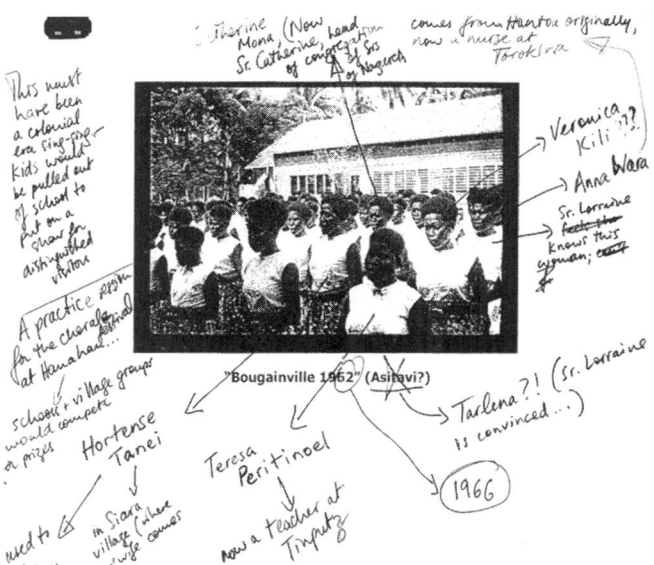

The author's annotated copy of Dr Allan Dwyer's 1966 photograph of the Tarlena Choir.

Even better, three years after this photo was taken, in 1969, when my father was back in Bougainville for a third trip, Catherine, Margaret and Elizabeth were no longer schoolgirls. It turns out they were working as nurses in the hospital at Tearouki, assisting my father in the operating theatre. So, they remembered him very well.

They also talked about a fellow called Jim Harding, whom I'd heard my mother mention on occasion. Now Jim, as I understand it, was a doctor at the Mater Hospital in Sydney, working with my father before training to become a priest and ending up as a missionary at Moratona in south-west Bougainville. He must have played an important role in persuading my father to go up there.

So, after hearing about Jim and Dad from the nuns, as soon as I got back from my 2004 trip, I went around to Mum's place—quick cup of tea, straight up into the attic, and there was this manila folder full of correspondence between my father and Jim Harding.

>PAUL *starts to read from one of the letters in the Jim Harding file:*

'The fourth of January 1967. Dear Allan, herewith the list of cases as promised…'

And there are the names of thirty-six patients upon whom my father performed surgery during the space of a few weeks in 1966…

>PAUL *resumes reading (and interpolates his own commentary on) the Jim Harding list:*

'Monowa, an eleven-year-old girl, Sovele mission area. Right wedge resection and tenotomy, fifth toe.'

'Laparopa, a six-year-old boy from the Sovele area. Bilateral medial release and TA'—which I've since found out is short for the 'Tibialis Anterior' muscle. That's the muscle that runs down the front of your shin and in this sort of situation…

>PAUL *gestures to the image* SEAN *has brought up on screen: a photo of a Bougainvillean boy's legs taken by Dr Dwyer senior.*

… sometimes you would have to lengthen the tendons that attach the muscle to the bone so that the patient can plant their heel properly.

'Moiku, a forty-year-old man from the Monoitu mission area, tenotomy flexors on the right arm'—this would have allowed Moiku to unfurl his arm so that he could grasp things and eat more easily. There's a note—in parentheses—'Moiku is very pleased'. Close parentheses.

'Poturoho, a fourteen-year-old boy from Monoitu mission, right triple arthrodesis'—arthrodesis is a word meaning 'fusion'—and it would be for a situation like this…

> PAUL *gestures to another image that has come up on the screen showing a child's feet that have 'rolled over'.*

… where the person can't walk. The top of your foot is not designed to support the weight of your body. You'll get stones and other sharp objects embedding themselves in your flesh, causing sores and tropical ulcers. But you can fuse together the bones in the ankle joint, so that the foot doesn't keep rolling over and the person can start to put weight through their ankle into the soles of their feet…

The nuns at Chabai described these operations to me in great detail. They also told me that my father was the first orthopaedic surgeon ever to visit Bougainville and, until recently, the only orthopaedic surgeon ever to visit. They speculated that other doctors might have been worried about having to perform surgery in the rudimentary conditions of the mission hospitals. 'But your father,' they told me, 'your father, Paul, worked with much less. The tools he brought were the tools of a carpenter—a hammer, a chisel, some nuts and bolts, screws, wire, a hacksaw.'

DAD'S HANDS

PAUL: My father had beautiful hands. It's what my mother always says: 'Dad had beautiful hands'. They get a mention here, too, in an article by the journalist Lou D'Alpuget who watched my father one time in the operating theatre.

> PAUL *goes to the display board, clicks on a third lamp, and reads:*

'Dr X'—my father wanted to be called Dr X—'is a man of medium height, of strong build, in his early fifties and as physically fit as a man half his age […] But the thing that continues to impress one is his gentle, modest manner. And his hands. They are broad and strong, with fingers that move expressively as he talks, the hands of a man who might also have been a pianist or a watchmaker.'[8]

It's a beautiful image but tempered, somewhat, for me by another strong image I have of Dad's hands… If he was driving us to school or to a footy match… It was a white Torana with a copper-topped roof. Some of you might remember those little triangular windows that were set into the corner of the main driver's side window, the ones you used to be able to push out sideways? So Dad would have his cigarettes in his top pocket. Push out the window, out comes the cigarette, reach for the lighter with the other hand, ashing out the window, sometimes chain-smoking…

He died of a cancer of the oesophagus less than two years after this article was written which, among other things, meant that 1969 was the last trip he made to Bougainville. He took siblings Number Seven and Eight on that trip—my brother Martin and my sister Genevieve. There are some lovely photos of the kids from that trip but more often you get this kind of image.

> SEAN *brings up on screen a slow montage of slides showing Dr Dwyer senior and the children in construction settings.*

My father's attention was being drawn towards the construction of the Panguna mine which was happening during the same period.

While his photos of the mine are of some archival significance, I have to say they don't really convey the true dynamism of what was a massive civil engineering project. To get a sense of that, we really couldn't go past the promotional film which was used by Bougainville Copper Limited (a subsidiary of Rio Tinto) and by the Australian administration to highlight the benefits of the mine for the peoples of Papua New Guinea and Bougainville (and, of course, for potential shareholders in Australia, the UK and elsewhere).[9] So, Sean, if you please…

VIDEO INTERLUDE: EXCERPT FROM MY VALLEY IS CHANGING

The opening images from the film show a young boy patiently sharpening a machete. He is seated in front of a thatched hut, among family. He then

THE BOUGAINVILLE PHOTOPLAY PROJECT

stores his machete away and runs down an enormous slope that has been cleared by bulldozers. As he reaches the bottom, where the bulldozers are now working, we hear his voice.

BOY: Thaddeus Nessico is my name. I like the bulldozers best. They have four gears forwards and four gears backwards. They are very beautiful. Here I used to grow a few pineapples. Now my valley is changing.

The image cuts to a shot of the central mountain ranges of Bougainville, filmed from the air.

VOICEOVER: And change comes hard to an island like Bougainville. An island that rises out of the Solomon Sea on the edge of the territory of Papua and New Guinea. An island where, until now, few men had reason to go.

The image dissolves from a Bougainvillean landscape to the streets of Melbourne, then cuts to the interior of a boardroom: four men in suits around a large desk, ashtrays, a secretary in the background taking notes.

VOICEOVER: In Melbourne, the chairman of Conzinc Rio Tinto of Australia, Sir Maurice Mawby, had a decision to make.

MAWBY: Good. How tough were the government in the negotiations, Frank?

FRANK ESPIE: Well, Canberra had a job to do, negotiating on behalf of a trust territory approaching independence, and they did it.

MAWBY: Do you think we conceded too much?

ESPIE: Well, not really, but we agreed an option over twenty percent of the equity at par on behalf of the local people and when we become taxable we'll be paying tax at about double the rate of other companies in the territory.

MAWBY: Well, let's face it. The original concept was that this would be a partnership between the company and the peoples of Papua New Guinea, with big benefits for both parties.

AN AMERICAN COLLEAGUE: Then there's the land question. The best we could get was a forty-two-year lease with an option for renewal.

MAWBY: And the government wants a director on the board?

AMERICAN: That's right

MAWBY: Anything else?

ESPIE: We've committed to a mighty big training program on behalf of the local people, but we're keen on that anyway.

MAWBY: Well, I suppose it's all part of setting up a copper mine of world class. At any rate, gentlemen, it looks as though we're in business.

Stirring music begins, accompanied by a montage of the mine construction. The imagery is heroic and energetic. Then there is a cut to images of villagers living by the beach.

VOICEOVER: A few miles north of Kieta live the Rorovana people. Their villages will not be affected by the project but they have a problem.

ROROVANA MAN: I am one of the Rorovanas. My people came from the Solomon Islands about eighty years ago in their canoes. Why they left the Solomons? Because they were fighting so much with the other people there. They plant something at Rorovana and stayed with their children and, now, the administration is wishing to take some of the land from us. We are very worried about our land.

Cut to a long shot of the land in question; this is followed by archival footage of a protest by the women of Rorovana.

VOICEOVER: This land. A two-hundred-acre strip where nobody lived but which was essential for the development of the multi-million dollar port. The land had been legally resumed but the women of Rorovana were not giving up without a protest. Just one survey peg was their mission and they got it. The battle was won, a token victory for the women of Rorovana.

End of the excerpt from My Valley is Changing.

ACKNOWLEDGEMENTS

PAUL: The women at Rorovana were after more than a token victory, of course. Most Bougainvillean societies are matrilineal, so these are the traditional landowners. They came back; they pulled out more survey pegs. When they did, the administration sent the native police in to beat them with sticks; they fired tear gas canisters into the crowd. This 'Rorovana Incident', as it became known, happened in 1969, about six months after my father's last trip to Bougainville. It was an event that galvanised a whole generation of Bougainvillean independence activists and clearly, in hindsight, was a portent of the violence to come.[10]

Fifteen to twenty thousand people died during the Bougainville crisis, either directly from combat or indirectly because there were no medicines getting through the blockade. That's roughly one in ten of the region's population. And this dirty, brutal, postcolonial war was bankrolled, largely, by Australia.[11]

We provided combat training for two thousand Papua New Guinea Defence Force personnel in far north Queensland. We provided the PNGDF with guns, ammunition, mortars, bombs, patrol boats, search planes and, most notoriously, four Iroquois helicopters. We paid a million dollars a year so that these helicopters could be serviced. They were flown by Australian pilots acting, basically, as mercenaries; and the PNGDF used them as helicopter gunships.

This was denied, of course, by all our political leaders. Bob Hawke, the prime minister at the time; Gareth Evans, the foreign minister; Paul Keating when he was treasurer—they all stood up in the Australian Parliament to dispute reports that these helicopters were being used for anything other than troop transportation and logistical support. But even PNGDF personnel were admitting the truth on Australian television and I can guarantee you that if you ask the people up here near Tinputz for example…

    PAUL *indicates on the map of Bougainville.*

… they will tell you exactly what it looks like to see a pastor and five of his parishioners abducted and driven down to Arawa, interrogated, taken out into the bush, shot dead in cold blood, loaded onto an Australian helicopter at Aropa airstrip, flown out over the reefs and dumped into the Pacific.[12]

MARILYN'S LIST

PAUL: During the worst of the crisis, there was a network of independence activists: Bougainvilleans in exile and their supporters, in the Solomons, New Zealand, the Netherlands, as well as Australia where, among others, there was Moses Havini and his wife Marilyn. They started getting what reports they could out of Bougainville concerning human rights abuses and Marilyn Havini compiled a dossier.[13]

> PAUL *is now sitting at the table downstage centre, the dossier in hand.*

I go through this documentation; time and again, I'm seeing the same names of villages that my father has scrawled in his slightly cramped handwriting across the bottom of his Kodachrome slides...

'Manetai area, Atomo Village, twenty-fifth April 1995, extra-judicial killing; Kotu Village, near Monoitu Catholic Mission, extra-judicial killing; Sovele area, Panam Village, Nagovis region, ambush, massacre, abduction...'

These are atrocities committed by the Papua New Guinea Defence Force, by members of the Bougainville Revolutionary Army, by Bougainvilleans in the Resistance militia, recruited by the PNGDF... The list goes on and on but, despite all this mounting evidence, it was proving extremely difficult to get traction for this story in the mainstream Australian media—with a few honourable exceptions, the ABC's Sean Dorney being one of them.

The Bougainvillean independence activists realised they needed photos to go with the story. Through contacts in the Solomons, they managed to smuggle into Bougainville, across the blockade, a package with some medicines and some disposable cameras, along with a message: 'If you see something, please, you must try to document it'. Thirty cameras went in; one came back.

MALABITA

PAUL: There's a place called Malabita in the south of Bougainville, near Buin where my father actually spent a lot of time. On the twenty-eighth of November 1996 the people of Malabita were let out of the 'care centre' into which they'd been corralled by the PNGDF to go to their local church. While they were praying, seven long-range mortar shells were fired from Malabita Hill straight into the church. Nine people were killed; many more were wounded. And that's what was documented on this one camera that came out.[14]

PAUL is sitting at the table downstage centre, holding a folder with the Malabita massacre images in it.

These are very difficult images. So we can do as before: I will give a verbal description of what I'm looking at before I ask Sean to bring anything up on the screen and you can decide for yourselves if now is the right time for you to be looking at these images.

So, I'm looking at a photograph with four bodies laid out on stretchers, made from bamboo slats. Some of them are covered by sheets; some are laid on top of the sheets. In the foreground there is a young boy wearing board shorts and a yellow shirt. There are blood strains all down the front of the shirt... Sean...

The image comes onto the screen.

The BRA provided the names of these victims: they are Alvina Mukunia, a six-year-old girl; Brenda Ruinai, a fourteen-year-old girl; Danny Makau, a five-year-old boy; and Boisi Kauri, a fifty-year-old woman.

I'm looking now at the image of a man's body, again on one of these makeshift stretchers. I can see his torso, his arms and hands but I cannot see his head; it's been blown off by a mortar shell... Sean.

Image on screen.

This is the body of Albert Makau, a forty-two-year-old man, and I'm guessing, from that surname, he's the father or perhaps an uncle of Danny Makau, the little boy from the previous photo.

In the next photo, I can see people have rolled some of these stretchers up and lashed them with vines; they're preparing the bodies for burial... Sean...

Image.

And I'm looking now at a photograph of the legs of a man who is lying on a stretcher that's been covered with banana leaves. His feet are on two cushions which are very blood stained; the right foot has been badly mutilated by mortar shell... Sean...

Image.

These are the legs of Francis Baubake, a thirty-nine-year-old man, and Francis is okay. The BRA got Francis and other survivors onto boats; they ran the blockade between Bougainville and the Solomons and got the wounded down to Honiara hospital where they were fixed up.

The Malabita massacre photos made the front page. They were published in the *Australian* and the *Sydney Morning Herald* and these images really did help to force the hand of the Australian government. We finally suspended the Defence Cooperation Agreement between Australia and PNG. Deprived of our military aid, the government of PNG tried to hire mercenaries—some of you might remember the Sandline affair? But when PNGDF troops, many of whom hadn't been paid for months, saw these well-heeled mercenaries fly in, they threatened to lead a mutiny on the streets of Port Moresby, and this, finally, was the moment when the PNG government accepted that there was no military solution to the Bougainville crisis.

PNG began to negotiate in good, or at least in better, faith with the Bougainvillean leadership. A peace agreement was struck that has held for over a decade. Bougainville is now an autonomous region within PNG. There is the promise of a referendum on independence to come some time in this decade. And now is also the time when Bougainvilleans, among themselves at least, are beginning to reconcile in extraordinary ways.[15]

SAMUEL'S LETTER (IS TENAI WALKING?)

PAUL: There's a letter here in the file of correspondence between my father and Jim Harding that I would like to share with you. It's a thankyou note to my father from a boy called Samuel Liombo, one of the patients Dad operated on in 1966. Samuel writes:

'Dear Dr Dwyer,

'*Mi say thank you long yu bikos yu bin stretim lek bilong mipala.* I want to say thank you because you fixed up our legs. *Nah mipala ken amamas taim mipala i wokabout gut.* And we can be really happy now when we're walking about okay. *Nah mi happy tumas long yutupala wantaim Father Doctor.* I'm really happy with you and the 'Father Doctor'—which must be a reference to Jim Harding. *Bikos em i gutpela job.* Because you did a good job. *Mipala i happy tumas taim mipala i lukim lek bilong mipala em i stret i pinis.* We're really happy every time we are looking at our legs because they are nice and straight, all fixed up. *Nah mipala i pein liklik.* But we do have a little bit of pain still. *Nah Tenai em i no wokabout.* And Tenai is not yet walking.'

According to Jim Harding's list, Tenai was a three-year-old boy who was operated on the day after Samuel Liombo, and I started thinking, 'Well, is Tenai walking now? What life did he, or any of the other patients on whom my father operated, walk into after my father had left, after the mine, after the crisis…?' Because it's very clear that my father would have wanted some kind of follow-up. There are other letters here in this file, six months, a year, sometimes two years after various operations, where Dad is corresponding with Jim Harding about particular patients. For instance: 'Dear Jim, the x-rays of the four hips arrived this morning. On the whole I think they will be satisfactory…' Detailed case notes. He wanted there to be post-operative follow-up.

THE BOUGAINVILLE PHOTOPLAY PROJECT *IN BOUGAINVILLE*

PAUL: Clearly, I'm not the kind of doctor who can offer that—a PhD is useful for some things but not all things, as I have learned. Still, I decided to return to Bougainville in 2007 and took with me a low-tech (well, really, a no-tech) version of *The Bougainville Photoplay Project*…

> DAVID *lowers from the flies a flip chart onto which large-format copies of the show's main slide images have been printed;* PAUL *starts flicking through them.*

My friend Russell rigged up this flip-chart for me that I could hang under a galip nut tree or under someone's house or in a marketplace and I'd go through a lot of the same stories and show many of the photos that we've been looking at tonight—

PAUL *stops on one image the audience hasn't seen before.*

This close-up image of the Rorovana incident always got a strong response in Bougainville; particularly the older people would start murmuring, '*Em nau, em nau...* that's where it starts...' Often they'd come up after the show and want to look again at this one and talk about where they were at the time. But...

PAUL *turns to another new image, in black and white: his father treating a Bougainvillean man's foot.*

To end the show in Bougainville, I used to stop on this image. For me, out of all the photos relating to my father's time in Bougainville, it's the one I love the most, although his caption for it is not particularly romantic: across the bottom of the slide he's written 'me and short-foot leper'. If you look closely, you can see that the man's toes are missing, so this must have been at Torokina on the south-west coast

Dr Allan Dwyer and a 'short-foot leper', Torokina, c.1962.

where there was a leper colony. I love the closeness, the sense of intimacy in this photograph. Of course, it's still a relationship that's mediated in all kinds of ways: by the history of the Catholic mission in Bougainville, the structures of colonialism and so on. Yet, it does seem as if, at least for this moment, my father and this Bougainvillean man had a pretty shared understanding of what was going on between them. It's about the foot. And this is not radical orthopaedic surgery; as far as I can tell, my father is simply applying a dressing to the man's wounded foot.

I would look at this photograph with audiences in Bougainville and I'd say to them something like: '*Dispela "relationship" em bruk, laga?* This relationship is broken, isn't it?' And they would say: '*Em nau.* That's right.'

'*Orait, hau bai yumi inap kirapim niupela "relationship" Australia wantaim Bogenvil? Hau bai yumi inap kirapim "reconciliation" Australia wantaim Bogenvil?* Can we make a new relationship, can we make some kind of reconciliation between Australians and Bougainvilleans?'

And they would say something like: 'Look, Paul, we're very happy to meet you. We're delighted to be reminded of the things your father did here, of some of the other good things that happened during the colonial period; that's great, you're welcome. But if you're talking about reconciliation between Australia and Bougainville, that's a very big question. Where are your leaders? Next time you come, you should come with your leaders, where are they?'

I couldn't answer that question. The best I could do was to volunteer to ask it of audiences in Australia. So?

The other thing I was hoping people in Bougainville could help me with was the John Berger question: 'How can we understand the value of a doctor's work? *Hau bai yumi inap skelim wok bilong wanpela dokta insait long komuniti bilong en?*' So I made an arrangement with Andrew Kuiai, the man from Peace Foundation Melanesia who was guiding me around Bougainville, that we would present the *Photoplay Project* in places as close as possible to the villages from where the patients in Jim Harding's 1966 list of patients had come.

> *Video documentation of* PAUL*'s 2007 Bougainville performances has started running silently on the upstage screens. Some of the footage is very dark; some of it is quite jerky.*

This was a fundraiser performance at Buka District Hospital. We had a power failure and had to continue the show by torchlight. This was in a classroom at Monoitu Catholic Mission. There's Andrew Kuiai, my guide from Peace Foundation; this is Mowo and this is Veronica Suru, former patients who appear on Jim Harding's 1966 list. And this is Anthony Poturoho—remember, the fellow with the 'right side triple arthrodesis'. I got to meet this man; it was extraordinary but also a little scary at first—he has one leg that's quite a bit shorter than the other and I was thinking, 'Oh, God, no, Dad must have stuffed up!' But he said, 'No, no, it's good. Before I was a cripple. People had to carry me everywhere. Now I can walk.' He's improvised a crutch for himself and goes bounding really fast along these bush tracks. It took me two and a half hours to walk up to his village to invite him to come and see my *'liklik Bogenvil Potopilai drama'* and I heard it only took him two hours the next day when he came down to Monoitu to see it. He's a great man, a man of culture; the people in the village told me he is one of the few who still goes hunting at night with a bow and arrow; he weaves beautiful traditional baskets…

I met Anthony, I met half a dozen of the people on Jim Harding's list and heard stories about a dozen more who are still alive and well. The Bougainville crisis did not destroy everything or everyone. But, still, all the time I was going around with Andrew Kuiai, I kept thinking about this fellow Tenai: is he walking? I think I'd been building Tenai up in my mind as some kind of Bougainvillean soul brother or something because, you know, Tenai was born in 1963 and I was also born in 1963; we have so much in common.

Then one day, Andrew Kuiai says to me, '*Tenai? Mi save long dispela man.* I know him. Laurence Tenai. *Em stap antap long mountain, antap long ples bilong mi.* His place is just a bit further up the mountain from my village. Would you like me to go find Laurence and invite him to come see your *liklik Potopilai drama*?'

'Yes, of course, Andrew. That'd be unreal!'

So he says, '*Okay, yumi wokim olsem dispela pasin.* Let's do it this way. You stay here tonight'—we were at Sovele Mission—'and I will walk up to my village, but that will take me about three hours and it will be dark by then so, if it's okay with you, I will stay and have dinner with my family and sleep in my own bed tonight'— which was fine by me (he hadn't seen his family in the two weeks that he'd been guiding me around)—'then I will get up early tomorrow morning and go straight up to the village of Laurence Tenai to see if he can come see your *liklik drama*.'

'*O tank yu tumas, Andrew. Mi amamas dispela pasin bilong yu bilong halivim mi.*'

'But you stay here, okay,' he says to me. 'Just stay here and you'll be fine.' And it was the first time in two weeks that he was leaving me on my own at night. He introduced me to a man called Peter Kobua ('*lapun Peter,* old Peter', Andrew called him) who he said would keep an eye out for me.

Okay, so '*Hello Peter. Nem bilong mi Paul...*' Andrew's heading off... '*Lukim yu Andrew!*'

NIGHT WALK TO MORATONA

PAUL: Then Peter Kobua says to me, 'I hear you have some interest in reconciliation?' 'Yes,' I tell him, '*Mi kam bilong wokim liklik "research".*'

'Okay,' says Peter, 'Did you know that there is going to be a big reconciliation ceremony tonight at Moratona?'

'Really!?' Moratona—that's where Jim Harding used to be based; that'd be so cool! 'Peter, are you planning on going to the reconciliation ceremony tonight?'

'*Nogat,*' he says to me, '*Mi no go.* But this man here will take you—'

'Oh, hello... Ah... *Nem bilong mi Paul. Nem bilong yu? Nem bilong yu Peter?* You're another Peter? So, Peter Kobua here, and now Peter...? Peter Kebono, here. Okay, right...'

And I'm shaking hands with Peter Kebono with the words from the Department of Foreign Affairs Travel Advisory Notice ringing somewhat loudly in my ears: 'Do not go out after dark in PNG under any circumstances'. But, well… *'Okay, Peter, yumi go!'*

I rush back to my room to top up my water…

> PAUL *drinks from a bottle next to* DAVID *at the tech desk.*

… top up my mosquito repellent.

> DAVID *sprays* PAUL.

It's getting dark but I have my torch. We go.

> *During the next few minutes, all the theatre's lights slowly fade to black; eventually, the stage is lit only by* PAUL's *torchlight.*

At first, the road is easy enough. Then we turn off onto what feels like an overgrown bush track. It's been raining hard in previous nights and there are places where you have to slosh through swollen creeks or where you're sinking into mud that goes almost up to your knees.

Peter Kebono is walking behind me. I think he wants to make sure that the *waitpela* man is not going to peg out on him. We've been going for about half an hour when I ask him, *'Peter, em longwe?* Is it a long way?' To which he replies, *'Em longwe liklik.* It's a little bit of a long way.' So I know it's going to be a very, very long way.

The rain also seems to have brought out this plague of frogs. The torchlight picks up their beady eyes, staring straight back at you, and they don't always hop off before the next footfall, which is rather disconcerting.

We're walking along; I've only just been introduced to this man and I'm thinking, 'Ethnographic fieldwork methodology, rule number one: establish rapport…' Okay. *'Peter, mi kam long Bogenvil bilong wokim liklik "research", bilong lanim pasin bilong yupela bilong wokim "reconciliation".'*

'Gutpela,' he says.

I give him the personal context too: *'Papa bilong mi bin kam long Bogenvil tu, long taim bipo, bipo long taim bilong crisis. Em bin kam bilong wokim sampela opersen long ol haus sik bilong ol katolik mission.'*

'*Gutpela tru*,' he says.

I feel like things are going okay, well enough at least for me to ask him what this reconciliation ceremony we are going to will be about. And so he starts explaining to me (in English—it turns out his English is very good):

'Well, Paul, you know during the crisis, we had the PNG Defence Force who did a lot of bad things; we had Bougainvilleans in the Resistance and in the BRA who did a lot of bad things. But we also sometimes had gangs, *raskols*, young men who would just go around taking advantage of the situation. They might call themselves BRA but they weren't really. They were what I would call "Skin BRA". From around this area, there were a couple of young men who were causing a lot of problems. They took offence at what some women from a nearby village were saying about them. They said the women were sorceresses, working black magic against them. So they kidnapped the women and held them prisoner for a long time, demanding a ransom. And, well, these boys—they are from my village, I'm their Paramount Chief. So we're going to try and reconcile over this matter.'

We walk on. He asks me, '*Paul, wanim dispela "salary cap"?*' He wants to know about the National Rugby League salary cap. I do my best to explain, slipping in a reference to the fact that I live near Leichhardt Oval, you know, home of the Wests Tigers. Still working on that ethnographic fieldwork rapport.

Then there's a moment where I can't hear or feel the presence of Peter Kebono behind me on the track anymore. And it is now quite dark. '*Peter? Peter? Peter yu stap we? Peter yu kam?*' Finally, there's this flash of white teeth coming out of the dark as he catches back up with me, saying, '*Em orait, yu no inap wori. Mi stap bilong changim batteries long torch bilong mi, tasol.*'

We walk on. Then we come to a place where Peter stops me. It just looks like any other bit of this track that we've been walking along but he holds me back. He says, 'Paul, did you know that we have snakes in Bougainville?' Which I didn't know. 'It's okay,' he says, 'they're not venomous but they do cause fear. So, these boys, they put snakes around the necks of the women; they made the women dance and kiss and fondle each other. Then they raped the women. They murdered them and this is where they threw the bodies. So we have to try and sort this one out.'

But he's telling me there will be other reconciliations too; this is not a normal ceremony; it's a special one; there will be lots of people coming to reconcile a whole lot of different matters. And I can tell we must be getting close to Moratona now because the track is starting to fill up with other people on their way to the reconciliation. Peter's introducing me to people: '*Yes, hello, nem bilong mi Paul... Hello, mi kam bilong wokim liklik "research"... Yes, hello, nice to meet you, mi kam long yunevesiti bilong Sydney...*'

We're moving up now onto this big plateau where the old Moratona mission is located. There must be about a thousand people here and this is not looking like 'traditional Bougainvillean reconciliation', quote unquote. There's a huge cross that's been erected in the open air and I ask Peter, 'What's with this cross?' 'Oh,' he says, 'you know World Youth Day? The Vatican? It's a bit like the Olympics when they have their torch relay. The Vatican sends a cross from Rome all around the world and it did come to PNG but only as far as Rabaul, East New Britain. It wasn't going to come to Bougainville, so some Bougainvillean artists, they went to Rabaul and they made a copy of the cross and brought it back to Bougainville so now we can do stuff with it, like what we're doing tonight.'

'Tonight,' he is telling me, 'this is just *"sek han reconciliation"*, just a shake of the hands.' There's too many people, too many things being reconciled; they're not roasting pigs and doing all the customary steps; groups of people are just lining up, one after the other, chewing betel nut, shaking hands, they keep coming up, the people are praying and chanting, there are these two choirs—the Moratona youth choir over here; the Sovele youth choir over here—these two choirs are just going off like duelling banjos or something, they're going—

    PAUL *breaks into song:*

> '*O Jisas, Jisas yu pren bilong mi!*
> *Halleluiah!*
> *Yu go antap, yu go antap tru. Jisas yu pren bilong mi!*
> *Halleluiah!*'

He stops, suddenly, in the middle of a crescendo.

'Peter, can this really work?'

'Yes,' he tells me, 'When the cross came to my village a few days ago, I just felt it was the right time. I walked down and I stood in front of it. I looked out into the crowd and said, "If the man is here tonight who killed my brother during the crisis, then I am ready to reconcile".' And apparently this guy just came out of the crowd, tears streaming down his face. They shook hands and they are reconciled.

These people have a culture of reconciliation and a commitment to it that goes so deep and, yes, they do have their traditional customs but they will take from other traditions too, they will splice stuff together, they will invent new rituals, they will do whatever is needed to get the job done. That night at Moratona was a long, strange and wondrous night.

CODA

PAUL: We got back to Sovele the next day and Andrew Kuiai, my guide, was there wagging a finger at me: 'You had a big night last night!' But I kind of felt chuffed, like I'd finally done the hard yards of ethnography…

'What about you, Andrew? *Yu bin painim Laurence Tenai?* Did you manage to find Laurence?'

'*Nogat,*' he says to me, '*Mi no bin painim em tasol yu bin lukim em.*'

'I would have seen him?'

'Yes,' he tells me, 'He was there last night at Moratona.'

'*Nogat!*'

'Yes, he would have been one of the people out the front, leading the whole ceremony, he's a catechist. You couldn't have missed him. He's really tall, like a basketball player.'

And there was this really tall guy out the front. I started describing him. And Andrew's going, '*Em nau, em nau.* That's him. That's the one!'

And on the way home to Sydney I remembered that I had taken a photograph at Moratona, just as dawn was breaking, when people were still lining up for reconciliation, when the tall guy was still out the front. I got back home, rushed to get the film in my disposable camera developed and...

> PAUL's Moratona *photo is projected on-screen; nothing is visible apart from the silhouette of trees against a dark blue dawn sky;* PAUL *points emphatically towards the middle of the image...*

Laurence Tenai is here.

> *A beat.* PAUL's *finger starts to trace a vague arc...*

Somewhere.

We didn't meet.

> *Tasol em orait. Bai mi go bek long Bogenvil. Ating bai mi save painim Laurence Tenai. Bai mi karim liklik presen i go long Laurence na famili bilong Laurence, ating sampela gutpela kaikai. Na mitupela i save sindaun na tokim sampela stori...*

I'm going back to Bougainville next year, with my wife Carmen and my two boys Frank and Tony. Well, that is to say I've entered into negotiations with my wife Carmen. Maybe it'll end up being just me, or just me and Frank... What I do know is that it is entirely possible to sit down with a man like Laurence Tenai and to learn what reconciliation means to him, how he sees it working in a rapidly changing Melanesian society, how he thinks perhaps it could work between Australia and Bougainville—after all, the man has expertise.

And after we've had our little research chat, maybe we could have a cup of tea, something to eat, share a few stories...

That's the plan for now. Thank you and goodnight.

NOTES

[1] On the parallels between contemporary western models of restorative justice and ritual traditions in various indigenous cultures, see John Braithwaite, 'Restorative justice and a better future'. *The Dalhousie Review* vol. 76, no. 1, pp. 9–31, 1997; and Pat Howley, *Breaking Spears and Mending Hearts*, Sydney: Federation Press, 2002. For a dissenting view, see Chris Cuneen, 'Restorative justice and the politics of decolonization' in *Restorative Justice: Theoretical Foundations*, edited by E. Weitekamp and H-J. Kerner, Cullompton, UK: Willan Publishing, 2002, pp. 32–49.

[2] *Breaking Bows and Arrows* was directed by Liz Thompson and produced by Ellenor Cox (Firelight Productions & Tiger Eye Productions, 2001). The film has screened on SBS TV in Australia and Vision TV in Canada, as well as at numerous international festivals. It was awarded the United Nations Media Peace Award for 2002. For more information and to purchase a copy: www.firelight.com.au/break1.html

[3] Adrian Lipscomb et al. *Papua New Guinea*, 6th edition, Melbourne: Lonely Planet Publications, 1998, p. 353. Since 2004, a new edition of this guide has appeared which, I note, takes an appropriately more positive view of travel in Bougainville.

[4] The voiceover here is from the audio recordings supplied with the text book by Thomas Dutton, *A New Course in Tok Pisin (New Guinea Pidgin)*, Canberra: ANU Press, 1985.

[5] Noel Newton, a general surgeon at the Mater Hospital in Sydney, and Arthur Sherwood, from Sydney University's Engineering Faculty, both contributed greatly to the development of the 'Dwyer technique' for treatment of scoliosis. Noel often performed the surgical entry through the patient's rib cage and Arthur designed many of the surgical instruments Noel and my father used. Their jointly authored article appeared in *Clinical Orthopaedics*, no. 162, pp. 192–202, 1969.

6. J-J. Rainaut, *Les Scolioses*, Paris: Ellipses, 1984, p. 267.
7. John Berger and Jean Mohr, *A Fortunate Man: The Story of a Country Doctor*, Harmondsworth: Penguin Books, 1969. The quoted material below is from pp. 164–165.
8. Lou d'Alpuget, 'Battery "welds" man's spine: brilliant work by Sydney surgeon', *The Sun*, 18 June 1973, pp. 1; 4; 12–13; 16–17. The quote is from p. 12. In the same newspaper, Lou D'Alpuget also published a front page story on my father's first use of the anterior approach to scoliotic surgery (17 August 1965) and an obituary (13 February 1975).
9. *My Valley is Changing*, directed by Lionel Hudson and produced by John Martin Jones and Roland Beckett, was an Australian Government-funded film first released in 1970. The film has recently been remastered and copies may be purchased from Screen Australia (www.screenaustralia.gov.au).
10. The 'Rorovana Incident' made headlines around the world, including detailed coverage in the *Sydney Morning Herald* (6, 7 and 8 August 1969). An excellent account, including transcripts of the tape-recorded reports filed by Australian officials overseeing the use of batons and tear gas, is also available in Donald Denoon, *Getting Under the Skin: The Bougainville Copper Agreement and the Creation of the Panguna Mine*, Canberra: Pandanus Books, 2000.
11. The causes, the contributions of various parties, and the consequences of the Bougainville crisis are understandably a matter of ongoing debate. It is clear, however, that training and military hardware provided to PNG by Australia under a broad Defence Cooperation Agreement allowed the PNGDF to prosecute its war against the BRA and also to arm the Resistance militia. One could argue that Australia never specifically approved the use of this military hardware for operations in Bougainville that resulted in gross violations of human rights but, even then, surely the question to ask is why Australia took so long to suspend the Defence Cooperation Agreement in the face of mounting evidence of such violations. The figures cited in this section of the show are drawn mainly from Naomi Sharp's report, *Bougainville: Blood on our Hands*, Sydney: Aid/Watch, 1997. Other useful, sometimes competing, accounts of the war can be found in Pat Howley's book (see note 1 above); in Josephine Sirivi and Marilyn Havini, eds., *As Mothers of the Land: The Birth of the Bougainville Women for Peace and Freedom*, Canberra: Pandanus Books: 2004; and in Anthony Regan and Helga Griffin, eds., *Bougainville Before the Conflict*, Canberra: Pandanus Books, 2005.
12. On the PNGDF's deployment of the Iroquois helicopters as 'helicopter gunships', and Australian denialism, see Mary-Louise O'Callaghan, *Enemies*

Within: Papua New Guinea, Australia, and the Sandline Crisis, Sydney: Doubleday, 1999; and Sean Dorney, *The Sandline Affair: Politics and Mercenaries and the Bougainville Crisis*, Sydney: ABC Books, 1998. The specific incident referred to in this section of the show occurred on St Valentine's Day, 14 February 1990: the murder of Pastor Raumo Benito, Siru Labatavi, Lazarus Gemon, Joe Siabea, Allan Mateari, Moiva Sibanai, whose bodies were later dumped into the sea, was reported by the *New Guinea Times* and Amnesty International.

[13] Marilyn Taleo Havini, ed., *A Compilation of Human Rights Abuses Against the People of Bougainville, 1989–1995*, Sydney: Bougainville Freedom Movement, 1995.

[14] The original photos of the Malabita massacre that I have in my possession are on loan from Moses and Marilyn Havini to whom I offer my sincere thanks for clarifying details of this event. Some of the photos are reproduced in the *Sydney Morning Herald* story of 16 December 1996.

[15] An excellent resource regarding the peace agreement and efforts towards reconciliation is the special journal issue edited by Andy Carl and Sr Lorraine Garasu, *Accord #12: Weaving Consensus: The Papua New Guinea-Bougainville Peace Process*, London: Conciliation Resources, 2002.

THE END

Belvoir presents a version 1.0 production

THE BOUGAINVILLE PHOTOPLAY PROJECT

Devised & Performed by **PAUL DWYER**
Director **DAVID WILLIAMS**

Belvoir's presentation of The Bougainville Photoplay Project opened at Belvoir St Theatre on 10 November 2010.

Video Artist **SEAN BACON**
Lighting Designer **FRANK MAINOO**
Technical Assistant **RUSSELL EMERSON**
Lighting Operator **TEEGAN LEE**

PRODUCTION THANKS Brigitte Angays, Sisters of the Congregation of Nazareth, Chabai (Srs Catherine, Elizabeth, Lorraine, Margaret), the Dwyer Family (Nano, Garrett, Terry, Denis, Damien, Mary, Patrick, Martin, Genny), Fr Jim Harding, the Havini Family (Moses, Marilyn, Taloi), Carmen Jarrett, Peter Kebua, Peter Kebono, Lalaga, Gay McAuley, Mark Mitchell, Mowo, Peace Foundation Melanesia (Andrew, Clarence, Gary, Rhoda), Anthony Poturoho, Mark Seton, Bernard Siarapi, Dr John Stephen, Veronica Suru, James Tanis, John Tompot, Richard Manner, Janine Peacock, Harley Stumm and the team at Performing Lines.

ACKNOWLEDGEMENTS Special thanks to Liz Thompson for permission to show footage from the documentary *Breaking Bows and Arrows*. For more information or to purchase a copy: **firelight.com.au/break1.html**

SUGGESTED FURTHER READING A. Carl & Sr L. Garasu (eds.), *Weaving Consensus: The PNG – Bougainville Peace Process. Accord 12* (2002); D. Denoon, *Getting Under the Skin: The Bougainville Copper Agreement and the Creation of the Panguna Mine* (2000); S. Dinnen (ed.), *A Kind of Mending* (2002); S. Dorney, *The Sandline Affair* (1998); P. Howley, *Breaking Spears and Mending Hearts* (2002); H. Laracy, *Marists and Melanesians* (1976); A. Regan & H. Griffin (eds.), *Bougainville Before The Conflict* (2005); J. Sirivi & M. Havini (eds.), *As Mothers of the Land* (2004); M. Wehner & D. Denoon (eds.), *Without A Gun* (2001).

COVER IMAGE Allan Dwyer
PHOTOGRAPHY Heidrun Löhr
DESIGN Alphabet Studio

WRITER'S NOTE

"[Losing land is like] taking the bones out of a man's legs, the man would not be able to walk." Unnamed villager, Bougainville, 1967

I met a man in Bougainville called John, from Hanahan village in Buka. John's party trick is to get you to feel his scalp, and then you realise he's got this massive scar all along the midline of his skull. He had his head split open with a bush knife by a "raskol", whose mates then chucked John in the back of a truck and drove him down to Arawa, planning to murder him. In the end they let him go, possibly thinking that he was going to die anyway from the head wound.

Not only did he survive; he has been through a reconciliation ceremony with the raskol who tried to kill him. When John is in Arawa he visits this young man and has stayed in his house; and when the man comes to Buka, John returns the favour. I find this story almost impossible to comprehend but without doubt, for the Australian citizens here among us, there is something to be learned from the people of Bougainville about how to do reconciliation – provided that we see ourselves as protagonists, and not simply spectators, of this process.

Paul Dwyer

DIRECTOR'S NOTE

It's October 2010, and I'm trawling through my old notebooks, looking for my notes of my first meeting with Paul Dwyer to discuss what eventually became The Bougainville Photoplay Project. In my tiny handwriting I find reams of rehearsal notes from the last six years of the now-casual, now-intense, now-languid periods of work that somehow conspired to create the beauty that is this show. But the precise target of my search – the very first extended discussion over too-many coffees in Ralph's Cafe at the University of Sydney in late 2004 – proves elusive. What I find instead are seemingly endless prompts for memory – my exhortations to remember particular things, things which, in the act of writing them down, I promptly forgot.

If nothing else, The Bougainville Photoplay Project is a performance about remembering. It's about the way in which memories accumulate, gather dust, and slip from mind. It's about the objects around which memory accretes, and the surprising acts of remembering that such objects can provoke. But of course at its heart, The Bougainville Photoplay Project is a performance about a very particular kind of remembering, the kind of remembering that acknowledges and begins to address past wrongs, particularly where these wrongs have been committed in Australia's name, with Australian assistance, and have then been actively forgotten by Australians. In taking stock of the past, with its complex entanglements of happy memories, good intentions, bad decisions, and avoidable tragedies, this kind of remembering might help to enable a new, shared future between our two nations.

This might seem to be an overly weighty ambition for a solo performance, but as Australian citizens and artists we have a responsibility to start somewhere. We're very glad to have you onboard for these acts of remembering, and we hope that you enjoy the journey.

David Williams

BIOGRAPHIES

PAUL DWYER
Deviser and Performer

Paul has worked as a performer / director on over a dozen major productions with youth and community theatre companies including MRPG, Freewheels and Shopfront. He was a founding member of the contemporary performance ensemble Public Works. Paul holds a Diplôme d'Etudes Approfondies in theatre from the University of Paris-8 and a PhD in Performance Studies from The Sydney University where he now teaches in the Department of Performance Studies. He is currently working on an ARC-funded study of restorative justice conferencing in NSW. He was the dramaturg for version 1.0's *Deeply Offensive and Utterly Untrue, From a Distance ... , The Wages of Spin* and *CMI (A Certain Maritime Incident)*.

DAVID WILLIAMS
Director

David is a performer, technician, director and writer. He is a founding member and CEO of version 1.0, and has co-devised and produced all of the company's work since 1998 including *The Bougainville Photoplay Project, This Kind of Ruckus, Deeply Offensive* and *Utterly Untrue, The Wages of Spin, CMI (A Certain Maritime Incident), From a Distance ...* and *The Second Last Supper*. He has worked with Sidetrack, Sydney Theatre Company, Blast Theory, Bonemap, and pvi collective. Parallel to this, he has worked as a mechanist and flyman at the Sydney Opera House since 1997. David holds an honours degree in theatre from University of Western Sydney Nepean, and a PhD from the University of New South Wales. David is currently an Honorary Associate at the University of Sydney, and has lectured in theatre at UWS and UNSW. He has scholarly articles published in *Australasian Drama Studies, Performance Paradigm* and *Research in Drama Education*, and his writings about contemporary performance appear regularly in *RealTime*.

SEAN BACON
Video Artist

Sean studied video at the University of Tasmania, graduating with First Class Honors in 1998. For Belvoir Sean was Video Designer and Operator for the 2010 production of *Measure for Measure*, and for version 1.0 *The Wages of Spin, Deeply Offensive and Utterly Untrue* and *This Kind of Ruckus*. From 2000 – 02 he worked with the French dance company Experience Harmaat, and their collaboration *Nobody Nevermind* opened the performance section of the 2001 Venice Biennial. Sean's other work include his solo shows *Collective* (Cast Gallery, Hobart) and *Brilliant Refraction* (Cube 37, Melbourne), and the collaborative performance pieces *Sleeplessness, Y.smith* (Karen Therese); and *Babel Project, The Bland Project* (Gravity Research Institute). In 2000 Sean had a four month residency at the Cité des Arts Paris and in October 2005 he undertook a three month residency at the Australia Council's Green Street Studios in New York City. Sean is currently completing his Masters in the use of live camera in interactive installation, performance and theatre at the University of New South Wales College of Fine Arts.

RUSSELL EMERSON
Technical Assistant

Russell is the Technical Director in the Department of Performance Studies, Sydney University. He has over thirty years professional experience working in theatre as a props maker, puppeteer, designer, video artist and production manager with a wide range of companies including Australian Theatre for Young People, Sydney Theatre Company, de Quincey Co. and version 1.0.

FRANK MAINOO
Lighting Designer

Frank completed his Performance degree in 2007 at the University of Wollongong in the fields of performing and production. For PACT Youth Theatre he has designed lighting for *Lotophagi: The Lotus Eaters*, *The Whale Chorus* and *The Three Minute Bacchae and Other Extreme Acts*. Frank is a founding member of Team Mess, devising and performing *Killing Don* (2009) and *This is it* (2010). For version 1.0 he was Stage Manager on the 2009 tour of *Deeply Offensive and Utterly Untrue*.

TEEGAN LEE
Lighting Operator

Originally from North Queensland, **Teegan** has been working in the entertainment industry and studying theatre in Sydney since 2003. She has worked across all areas of production including independent theatre, corporate events, commercial musicals, international arts festivals and main stage subsidised theatre. Teegan's main focus is lighting and her design credits include *The End* (Belvoir); *Yellow Moon* (B Sharp / White Blackbird Productions); *The Suicide*, *The Only Child* (B Sharp / The Hayloft Project); *The Dysfunkshonalz* (Arts Radar / Darlinghurst Theatre Company); *A Couple of Poor Polish Speaking Romanians* (Focus Theatre); *Crave, Lot's Wife* (AbitOnTheSide Productions); *The Kitchen* (NIDA); *Insert Comedy* (Melbourne International Comedy Festival); *Improcaylpse Now*, *Old Fashioned Standards* (Studio Four); and *12 Angry Men* (Canned Laughter).

BELVOIR

Belvoir sprang into being out of the unique action taken to save the Nimrod Theatre building from demolition in 1984. Rather than lose a performance space in inner city Sydney, more than 600 arts, entertainment and media professionals as well as ardent theatre lovers, formed a syndicate to buy the building. The syndicate included nearly every successful person in Australian theatre.

Belvoir is one of Australia's most celebrated theatre companies. Under the artistic leadership of Neil Armfield, the company performs at its home at Belvoir St Theatre in Surry Hills, Sydney, and from there tours to major arts centres and festivals both nationally and internationally. Belvoir engages Australia's most prominent and promising playwrights, directors, actors and designers to present an annual artistic program that is razor-sharp, popular and challenging.

Belvoir St Theatre's greatly loved Upstairs and Downstairs stages have been the artistic watering holes of many of Australia's great performing artists such as Geoffrey Rush, Cate Blanchett, Susie Porter, Richard Roxburgh, Max Cullen, Bille Brown, David Wenham, Deborah Mailman and Catherine McClements.

Landmark productions like *Cloudstreet*, *The Diary of a Madman*, *The Alchemist*, *Hamlet*, *Waiting for Godot*, *Gulpilil*, *The Sapphires*, *Stuff Happens*, *Keating!*, *Parramatta Girls*, *Exit the King*, *Who's Afraid of Virginia Woolf?*, *Toy Symphony*, *The Book of Everything*, *Page 8* and *Gwen in Purgatory* have consolidated Belvoir's position as one of Australia's most innovative and acclaimed theatre companies. Belvoir also supports outstanding independent theatre companies through its annual B Sharp season.

Belvoir's 2011 Season marks Ralph Myers's first year as Artistic Director.

BELVOIR STAFF

18 Belvoir Street, Surry Hills NSW 2010
Email mail@belvoir.com.au **Web** www.belvoir.com.au
Administration (02) 9698 3344 **Facsimile** (02) 9319 3165 **Box Office** (02) 9699 3444

Artistic Director 2010
Neil Armfield AO

Artistic Director 2011
Ralph Myers

General Manager
Brenna Hobson

BELVOIR BOARD
Louise Herron (Chair)
Neil Armfield AO
Anne Britton
Andrew Cameron
Peter Carroll
Michael Coleman
Gail Hambly
Rachel Healy
Brenna Hobson
Frank Macindoe

BELVOIR ST THEATRE BOARD
Trefor Clayton (Chair)
Jane Jose
Stuart McCreery
Ralph Myers
Angela Pearman
Nick Schlieper
Kingsley Slipper

ARTISTIC AND PROGRAMMING
Resident Director
Simon Stone
Associate Director – New Projects
Eamon Flack

Associate Artists 2010
Wayne Blair
Susanna Dowling
Sarah John
Cristabel Sved

Associate Artist 2011
Stefan Gregory

Downstairs Theatre Director
Annette Madden

B Sharp Coordinator
Tahli Corin

EDUCATION
Acting Education Manager
Cathy Hunt
Education Coordinator
Tahni Froudist

ADMINISTRATION
Artistic Administrator
John Woodland
Administration Coordinator
Pearl Kermani

FINANCE & OPERATIONS
Head of Finance & Operations
Richard Drysdale
Financial Administrator
Ann Brown

Accounts Payable
Fiona Matthews
IT & Operations Manager
Jan S. Goldfeder

BOX OFFICE
Box Office Manager
Nicole Traynor
Assistant Box Office Managers
Tanya Ginori-Cairns
Alana Hicks

FRONT OF HOUSE
Front of House Manager
Damien Storer
Acting Assistant Front of House Manager
Alex Bryant-Smith

DEVELOPMENT
Development Manager
Katy Wood
Partnerships Coordinator
Zoë Hart
Philanthropy Coordinator
Shauna Wolifson

MARKETING
Acting Marketing Manager
Nathalie Vallejo
Acting Marketing Coordinator
Tahni Froudist
Publicist
Meera Hindocha
Publications Coordinator
Stephen Asher

PRODUCTION
Production Manager
Hall Murray
Technical Manager
Chris Page
Production Deputy
Glenn Dulihanty
Resident Stage Manager
Mark Lowrey
Construction Manager
Govinda Webster
Costume Coordinator
Judy Tanner
Downstairs Technical Managers
Teegan Lee
Jack H. Audas Preston

BELVOIR DONORS

We give our heartfelt thanks to all our donors for their loyal and generous support.

FOUNDATION DONORS

The measure of any great theatre is its capacity to provide a strong foundation for its long-term renewal. The following major donors have made a significant financial investment in the Belvoir Creative Development Fund, which supports artistic development beyond the demands of our annual season and budget.

Neil Armfield AO
Anne Britton
Andrew Cameron
Janet & Trefor Clayton
Anne & Michael Coleman

Hartley & Sharon Cook
Leon Fink
Gail Hambly
Anne Harley
Hal Herron

Clark Butler &
Louise Herron
Victoria Holthouse
Helen Lynch
Frank Macindoe

Ann Sherry &
Michael Hogan
Mary Vallentine AO
Kim Williams AM

THE CHAIR'S GROUP

This group provides special support for the development and staging of Indigenous theatre at Belvoir and enhanced opportunities for many Indigenous artists. Members of the 2010 Chair's Group are:

Anonymous (3)
Antoinette Albert
Jillian Broadbent AO
Louana Butler
Jan Chapman
Louise Christie

Warren Coleman &
Therese Kenyon
Kathleen & Danny Gilbert
Marion Heathcote &
Brian Burfitt
HLA Management Pty Ltd
Belinda Hutchinson AM

The Jarzabek Family
Cassandra Kelly
Hilary Linstead
Wendy McCarthy AO
Jillian Segal AM
A.O. Redmond
Ann Sherry AO

Victoria Taylor
Penny Ward
Kim Williams AM
Catherine Yuncken

B KEEPERS

Our B Keepers play a vital role within the company. B Keepers are a unique group of individuals whose financial support, often over many years, is a reflection of their passion for and commitment to Belvoir. Income received from B Keepers underpins all of our activities. Our 2010 B Keepers are:

Corporate B Keeper:
Sterling Mail Order
Macquarie Group Foundation

Anonymous (7)
Robert & Libby Albert
Gil Appleton
John Sharpe &
Claire Armstrong
Berg Family Foundation
Bev & Phil Birnbaum
Max Bonnell
Mary Jo & Lloyd Capps
Brian T. Carey
Elaine Chia
Jane Christensen
Louise Christie

Peter Cudlipp &
Barbara Schmidt
Suzanne &
Michael Daniel
Chris & Bob Ernst
Jeanne Eve
Peter Fay
Margaret Fink
A. & R. Maxwell
Peter Graves
David & Kathryn Groves
David Haertsch
Wendy & Andrew Hamlin
Beth Harpley
John Head
Marion Heathcote &
Brian Burfitt
Michael & Doris Hobbs
Peter & Jessie Ingle

Rosemary &
Adam Ingle
Anita Jacoby
The Jarzabek Family
Avril Jeans
Rosemarie &
Kevin Jeffers-Palmer
Margaret Johnston
Rob & Corinne Johnston
Phil Kachoyan
Colleen Kane
A. le Marchant
Jennifer Ledgar &
Bob Lim
Hilary Linstead
Stephanie Lee
Atul Lele
Prof. Elizabeth More AM
Dr David Nguyen

D. & L. Parsonage
Timothy & Eva Pascoe
Richard &
Heather Rasker
Greg Roger
Geoffrey Rush
Peter & Jan Shuttleworth
Edward Simpson
Judith & Howard Smith
Rob & Julie Smith
Chris & Bea Sochan
Victoria Taylor
Sue Thomson
Brian Thomson &
Budi Hernowibowo
Dr Orli Wargon
Alison M Wearn
Paul & Jennifer Winch
Iain & Judy Wyatt

EDUCATION DONATIONS

Thank you to our Education donors who help us to provide opportunities for young people throughout NSW to access Belvoir's unique work.

Anonymous (10)
Alexander Belford
Jan Burnswoods
Richard Cogswell
Rev. Cannon Warren Croft
Sandra Gross
Sophie Guest
Julie Hannaford
Jan Harland
John Harrison
Michael & Doris Hobbs
Paul & Melissa Hobbs
Dorothy Hoddinott
Susan Hyde
Shirley Jarzabek
Stewart & Jillian Kellie
Jacqueline Kott
Robyn Kremer
Jennifer Ledgar &
Bob Lim
Ken Leonhardt
Peter Levett
Ross Littlewood
Jim & Michael McAlary
Julie Mills
Elizabeth Meyer
Patricia Novikoff
Craig Pearce
Louise Roxburgh
Janet Ryan
Sandra See
Peter & Jan Shuttleworth
Kerry Stubbs
Jennifer Symons
Victoria Taylor
Shirley Treloar
Carolyn Wright
Jane Westbrook
Peter White
Murray Wilcox

GENERAL DONATIONS OVER $100

We thank the patrons, who, through general donations to Belvoir, provide valuable support to the projects most in need throughout the year.

Anonymous (21)
Annette Adair
Ross Armfield
Sandra Lim &
Phillip Arnold
Prof. Marie Bashir AC CVO
Susan Bennett
Peter Best
Jennifer Bott
Kathy & David Bradley
Mary Burchell
Andrew Cameron
Colleen &
Michael Chesterman
Tracey Clancy
Victor Cohen
Dayn Cooper
Bryony & Timothy Cox
Alan & Catherine Cunningham
Jennifer Darin
Dr Susan Davenport
Vivianne De Vahl Davis
Jane Diamond
Anne Duggan
Bruce Dunbar
Margaret Dunlop
Sol Encel
Kathryn Estitt
Carole Ferrier
Dr Ronald Lee Gaudreau
Helen Thwaites & Peter Gray
Priscilla A. M. Guest
Diane Hague
Louise Hamshere
Anthony Harris
Libby Higgin
Harrison & Kate Higgs
Ailsa Hocking
Vernon &
Margaret Ireland
Robert Jackson
Robert Jenssen
Colin & Connie Jessup
Gordon Johnson
Gloria Jones
Richard T. Jones
Despina Kallinikos
Michael &
Silvia Kantor
Bob Kijurina
Jacqueline Kott
Robyn &
Andrew Kremer
Mark Lalor &
Terry O'Neill
Carol Lack
Elizabeth &
Colin Laverty
John Lewis
Ross Littlewood
Sally Lomax
Catherine L'Estrange &
Louise-Anne Louw
Wailyn Mar
Phil & Jenny Marchionni
David & Vasantha Martin
Ingrid Storm &
Kevin McCreton
Jo Millyard
Dr Peter & June Musgrove
Peter Murray
Alison Nation
Patricia Novikoff
Anne O'Driscoll
Janette Parkinson &
Roy Fernandez
Geoff & Judy Patterson
Jocelyn Plate
Bertram Rosenberg
Shefali S. Rovik
Katherine Samaras
Beverley Sarvay
J.C. Savage
Catriona Simson
Agnes E. Sinclair
Eileen Slarke
Jean Smail
Deborah Stow
Augusta Supple
Lee Tanabe
Carmel Taylor
Helen Thompson
Judy Thomson
Douglas Trengove
Chris Vik & Chelsea Albert
Edwina Waddy
John & Gail Ward
Sarah Walters
Lynne Watkins &
Nicholas Harding
Ellen Waugh
Harold & Gwenda Welsh
Neil & Jill Wilson
Carolyn Wright

Belvoir is very grateful to accept all donations. Donations over $2 are tax deductible. If you would like to make a donation, or would like further information about any of our donor programs please call our Development Manager Katy Wood on (02) 8396 6224 or email katy@belvoir.com.au

ABOUT VERSION 1.0 INC.

version 1.0 inc. is an ensemble of artists who make performance through collaboration, investigating and also enacting democracy. We make devised performances that are both political and intensely personal, based on strong research, and that engage with significant political and social issues using innovative theatrical strategies. version 1.0 is acclaimed across Australia for our innovative, accessible, and entertaining blend of documentary theatre, contemporary performance, and media spectacle. Previous performance works includes the widely acclaimed *Seven Kilometres North-East* (2010), *The Bougainville Photoplay Project* (2008 – 2010), the Helpmann Award-winning *This Kind of Ruckus* (2009 – 2010), the Drovers Award-winning *Deeply Offensive and Utterly Untrue* (2007 – 2009), *The Wages of Spin* (2005 – 2006), and *CMI (A Certain Maritime Incident)* (2004). Founded in 1998, version 1.0 was granted Key Organisation status as an Artistic Explorer by the Theatre Board of Australia Council for the Arts in 2009.

versiononepointzero.com

STAFF AND ARTISTS
CEO Dr David Williams
General Manager Jocelyn Payne
Company Artists Danielle Antaki, Sean Bacon, Stephen Klinder, Jane Phegan, Christopher Ryan, Dr Yana Taylor and Kym Vercoe
Associate Artist Deborah Pollard
Company Dramaturg Dr Paul Dwyer

COMMITTEE OF MANAGEMENT
Dr Hillary Ray (President)
Dr Bryoni Trezise (Vice President)
Neil Adams (Treasurer)
Janine Collins
Richard Drysdale
Christopher Ryan
Kym Vercoe (Secretary)

VERSION 1.0 INC.
Level 2, Carriageworks
245 Wilson Street
Redfern NSW 2016
Phone: +61 2 8571 9082
Email: admin@versiononepointzero.com
Web: www.versiononepointzero.com

version 1.0 inc. is supported by the Australian Government through the Australia Council, its arts funding and advisory body, and by the NSW Government through Arts NSW. This project is also assisted by the Department of Performance Studies at the University of Sydney

version 1.0 inc. would like to thank the generous support of our 2010 donors:
Steve Fitts and Janine Collins, David and Vivian Williams, Dr Hillary Ray, Neil Adams, Dr David Williams, Sarah Miller, Fiona Winning, Julieanne Campbell and Dr Meg Mumford

Without your support version 1.0 would not be able to continue making cutting-edge art that matters, and performance that opens spaces for public conversation.
To make a tax-deductible donation and become part of version 1.0's future, please visit our secure online donation portal at **givenow.com.au/versiononepointzero**

Coming Soon to the Downstairs Theatre

A DISTRESSING SCENARIO
A DOUBLE BILL BY POST AND VERSION 1.0

PART ONE: *Everything I Know About the Global Financial Crisis in One Hour* by post
DEVISED / PERFORMED BY
ZOE COOMBS MARR
MISH GRIGOR
NATALIE ROSE

PART TWO: *The Market is Not Functioning Properly* by version 1.0
DEVISED / PERFORMED BY
JANE PHEGAN
KYM VERCOE

DIRECTED BY DAVID WILLIAMS
VIDEO ARTIST SEAN BACON
PRODUCTION MANAGER & LIGHTING DESIGNER
FRANK MAINOO

25 NOVEMBER – 19 DECEMBER
BOOKINGS 02 9699 3444 BELVOIR.COM.AU/SCENARIO

SILVER SPOON
CATERERS

Caterers for Belvoir and Opera Australia

9417 3878

jenniedelisle@silverspoon.net.au

www.silverspoon.net.au

THE DIARY OF A MADMAN

By NIKOLAI GOGOL
Adapted by DAVID HOLMAN,
NEIL ARMFIELD and GEOFFREY RUSH
Director NEIL ARMFIELD

Music By ALAN JOHN
(after Mussorgsky)
Set Designer CATHERINE MARTIN
Costume Designer TESS SCHOFIELD
Lighting Designer MARK SHELTON
Sound Designer PAUL CHARLIER

With GEOFFREY RUSH and YAEL STONE
Musicians PAUL CUTLAN and ERKKI VELTHEIM

4 – 23 DECEMBER 2010
2 JANUARY – 6 FEBRUARY 2011
BOOKINGS 02 9699 3444 OR
BELVOIR.COM.AU/DIARY

belvoir 2011

The Wild Duck
By Henrik Ibsen
Director Simon Stone
12 FEBRUARY – 27 MARCH

Jack Charles v the Crown
By Jack Charles & John Romeril
Director Rachael Maza Long
30 MARCH – 17 APRIL

Cut
By Duncan Graham
Directed by Sarah John
7 APRIL – 1 MAY

The Business
Based on *Vassa Zheleznova* by Maxim Gorky
Adapted by Jonathan Gavin with Cristabel Sved
Director Cristabel Sved
23 APRIL – 29 MAY

The Kiss
By Anton Chekhov, Kate Chopin, Peter Goldsworthy and Guy De Maupassant
Director Susanna Dowling
12 MAY – 5 JUNE

The Seagull
By Anton Chekhov
Director Benedict Andrews
4 JUNE – 17 JULY

Neighbourhood Watch
By Lally Katz
Director Simon Stone
23 JULY – 28 AUGUST

Windmill Baby
By David Milroy
Director Kylie Farmer
28 JULY – 21 AUGUST

Human Interest Story
Choreographer Lucy Guerin
31 AUGUST – 18 SEPTEMBER

And They Called Him Mr Glamour
By Gareth Davies
Director Thomas Wright
15 SEPTEMBER – 9 OCTOBER

Summer of the Seventeenth Doll
By Ray Lawler
Director Neil Armfield
24 SEPTEMBER – 13 NOVEMBER

The Dark Room
By Angela Betzien
Director Leticia Cáceres
3 – 27 NOVEMBER

As You Like It
By William Shakespeare
Director Eamon Flack
19 NOVEMBER – 24 DECEMBER

SEDUCTIVE	FURIOUS
BASHFUL	CHEEKY
JEALOUS	STERN

At Optus, we know our role in theatre.

OK, so Optus may not be the world's finest thespians. But we do know how to make theatre possible for everyone, through our special collaboration with Belvoir. Our unique 'Charitable Tickets' and 'Unwaged Performance Programs' offer free tickets to those who rarely have the opportunity to enjoy the theatre.

BELVOIR THANKS

CORPORATE PARTNER

PARTNER

IT PROJECTS PARTNER

MAJOR SPONSORS

ASSOCIATE SPONSORS

EVENT SPONSORS

ElBulli Spanish Tapas   VINI

Bird Cow Fish, Coopers, One Earth Foods, Silver Spoon Caterers

GOVERNMENT PARTNERS

SUPPORTERS

The Coca-Cola Australia Foundation, The Ian Potter Foundation, Macquarie Group Foundation, Matana Foundation for Young People, Media Tree, Michael Corridore Photography, Sidney Myer Fund, Thomas Creative, Teen Spirit Charitable Foundation, managed by Perpetual

For more information on partnership opportunities please contact our Development Manager Katy Wood on (02) 8396 6224 or email katy@belvoir.com.au

www.currency.com.au

Visit the Currency Press website now to:

- Buy your books online
- Browse through our full list of titles, from plays to screenplays, books on theatre, film and music, and more
- Choose a play for your school or amateur performance group by cast size and gender
- Obtain information about performance rights
- Find out about theatre productions and other performing arts news across Australia
- For students, read our study guides
- For teachers, access syllabus and other relevant information
- Sign up for our email newsletter

The performing arts publisher